The Best of 24 HOURS

The Best of 24 HOURS

✦

New Ten-Minute Plays

Edited by Scot Lahaie

iUniverse, Inc.

New York Lincoln Shanghai

The Best of 24 HOURS
New Ten-Minute Plays

iUniverse books may be ordered through booksellers or by contacting:

iUniverse
2021 Pine Lake Road, Suite 100
Lincoln, NE 68512
www.iuniverse.com
1-800-Authors (1-800-288-4677)

ISBN-13: 978-0-595-35066-7 (pbk)
ISBN-13: 978-0-595-79772-1 (ebk)
ISBN-10: 0-595-35066-6 (pbk)
ISBN-10: 0-595-79772-5 (ebk)

Printed in the United States of America

Contents

Preface

The ten-minute plays in this collection were originally staged at Gardner-Webb University in Boiling Springs, North Carolina. They were created in an event called 24 HOURS, in which our theater students are challenged to write, rehearse, stage, build, and perform six new ten-minute plays in a single twenty-four-hour period. The scripts in this collection are the best of the five staged events I have supervised over the past two-and-a-half years. This event, which is held once each semester at GWU, has become an outrageously successful event and never fails to fill the theater. Requests for performance rights for these plays should be made to the playwrights directly, when possible. The editor will happily assist in connecting the playwrights with potential performance venues.

Although the express purpose of this performance event is to train students in the craft of theater production, we have been pleasantly surprised by the quality of scripts our students have produced in the crucible-of-fire that this action-packed event creates. It is because of this unexpected bi-product that I am publishing the work of my students. I believe you will agree with me that these scripts compete neck-and-neck with plays in similar collections. Members of our local audience enjoy the excitement generated by our 24 HOURS event. Indeed, we regularly receive feedback from our audiences expressing their appreciation for the work we do in our new-work venues.

To give our readers a better appreciation of the creative energy let loose in this performance event, I will explain the proceedings of our particular venue, knowing that there are similar events around the country, both professional and educational. Since 24 HOURS always performs on a Saturday evening, we begin our process on Friday evening at 7:00 PM. We begin with a company meeting, at which time roll is called, newcomers are introduced, and the schedule is explained. Once everyone is working from the "same sheet of paper," as it were, we dismiss actors, directors, and technicians. Twelve writers remain in the theater and are assigned a stage prop. They are required to either write the play around the assigned prop or to include the prop in the play in a significant fashion. This prevents our playwrights from working out their scripts in advance, which would of course take away the fun of writing under pressure. Once the twelve writers have their props in hand, they scatter throughout the facility seeking a comfortable (if not quiet) place to write. As both producer and educator, I require my students to craft their scripts using a pen or pencil and notebook paper. We have experimented with composing on the computer, but I have been very dissatisfied with the results. The creative process belongs to the right side of the brain; operating a computer keyboard engages the left side of the brain. Trying to write creatively with the left brain functions engaged seems to restrict the creative process for many of my students. Typically, the first pen-and-paper drafts are finished between 9:00 PM and 11:00 PM. The writers then report to the computer lab to type up their drafts. It is at this point that my job becomes more hands-on.

As producer, dramaturge, editor, and teacher, it is my job to select six of the twelve scripts that I feel have the most potential for reaching the stage the next evening. Sometimes I will find scripts that are so clean, there is not much else to do to them. Sometimes I find scripts that have potential, but have gotten lost along the way. Some scripts make too many demands for scenic, costume, or property elements and are thus set aside; other scripts resemble screenplays and are left behind. Once I have completed reading the typed scripts, I gather the writers together to tell them of my decisions. Six writers rejoice; six writers heave a sigh. Such is the life of a writer. After this announcement, I pair each of the six writers whose work was selected with the six whose work was rejected. In groups of two, they return again to the proverbial drawing table in order to polish the selected plays. They read the work aloud, discuss character motivation, identify rising action and climaxes, and polish dialogue. Once satisfied with their second drafts, the writers bring me their work for another reading. This working together has saved us a lot of grief. Indeed, I ascribe much of the success of our event to this writer/dramaturge collaboration. After the second reading, I usually become very specific with the writers about what needs to happen to bring the script to finished copy. A third and fourth draft result from my comments. Once I am satisfied that the script is ready for a director, we print off copies for the director, designer, and the actors, and the writers head home for a couple of hours of sleep. It is not unusual for our writers to return the next morning to direct or act in the plays. The last scripts are typically completed around 4:00 AM.

The next morning around 6:00 AM, the directors arrive and get their scripts—some are chosen, while others are assigned. (More demanding scripts are assigned to our more experienced student directors.) The directors have only two hours to read and analyze their scripts, which is not a lot of time to figure out what makes a script work. It is, however, all they have. Auditions begin at 8:00 AM in the main hall. The audition, which is usually just a cold reading, is often chaotic. As they read from the first script, they are being considered for all the scripts. We do not have time to have everyone read from every script; we see everyone once. The directors then gather at 9:30 AM to discuss their casting choices. We often discover that several actors are wanted by multiple directors. Through quick but painful acts of compromise we resolve our casting issues and announce the casts before 10:00 AM. The casts report immediately to their rehearsal spaces and begin their first readings; thus the rehearsal marathon begins. With any luck, they are 'off book' and 'blocked' before 2:00 PM.

On the technical front, scripts are given to the technical director upon his early arrival. Each of the plays is assigned a technical liaison to coordinate sets, props, costumes, and light requirements for the specific plays. One play required a bus stop sign; it was fabricated from the scene shop. One play required a large Nazi flag; it was constructed in the costume shop in a matter of hours. One play required an office cubicle; it was borrowed from a local office and hauled across town in a volunteer's pick-up truck. Lights are hung, sound cues are recorded, and costumes are fitted. Panic sets in as the clock ticks away the hours. At 4:00 PM on Saturday, technical rehearsals begin. Each of the six plays is given thirty minutes on stage to work out the details of set-up, strike, and cues. It is seldom enough time.

With so little sleep and so much to do in just twenty-four hours, nerves run thin as we approach a 7:30 PM curtain. The audiences begin lining up around 7:00 PM. The energy surrounding the event is electric for both audience and actors. Makeshift programs are printed and handed out to the audience as they enter the space at 7:15 PM. With a short prayer, the actors in the first show take their places backstage. I give a curtain speech explaining our process to the audience. Many have heard it before and are returning for more. I tell our audience that putting on a play in just twenty-four hours is like "dancing on the rim of a volcano! You might have a great and glorious dance, but, then again, you might just fall in and burn up. Such is the nature of this exciting event." The audience laughs. If they only knew… if they only knew! One after another, the plays take their turn until the evening is finished. The applause is heard; the event is complete. Now we sleep.

24 HOURS is just one of three events sponsored by Gardner-Webb University Theater that is dedicated to the development of new plays. We also host the annual *New Plays Festival* each spring and a *Playwright's Workshop* each fall. The first of these two programs encourages emerging dramatists from across the nation by staging their short plays and providing feedback during and after the production process. We also publish these new plays as a means of sharing the work of these developing dramatists. Volumes one and two of our *New Plays Festival: New Plays by Emerging American Playwrights* are presently on the market; Volume Three of this series is due out in summer 2005. Also, each fall our *Playwright's Workshop* stages a new full-length play with the playwright present on campus to assist with rewrites and development. My own play *Dogfall* (exploring the ethical questions surrounding doctor-assisted suicide and the right-to-die movement) was the 2003 selection for this workshop. I am happy to report that this play subsequently won multiple awards, to include the Charles M. Gretchel New Play Award from SETC, the Mark Gilbert New Play Award from the Greensboro Playwrights' Forum, and the New Play Award from NCTC. Further information about our programs can be found online at theater.gardner-webb.edu.

Scot Lahaie
Director of Theater
Gardner-Webb University
March 2005

Acknowledgements

This volume is dedicated to my students, friends, and colleagues at Gardner-Webb University who contributed to the development of these plays through their hard work and fine insights. It has been my privilege to work together with you in the ancient art of the theater. You are the best! It is also with much appreciation that I thank Joyce Lahaie for proofing the manuscript on its way to the publisher.

S. L.

Equal Opportunity Employer

by Rachel Jones
with Carrie Cranford

Equal Opportunity Employer

by Rachel Jones
with Carrie Cranford

THE CHARACTERS

Katie Morrison—A talent agent.
Wallace Carris—An independent talent agent.
Tracy Oliver—Katie's supervisor at the agency.

THE SCENE

The Setting: Katie Morrison's office at the talent agency.
The Time: The present.

(At lights up, we see KATIE in a business suit sitting behind her desk. TRACY enters. She carries a portfolio with interview papers. WALLACE follows her into the room. He carries a briefcase.)

TRACY

Ms. Morrison?

KATIE

Yes. Hello, Ms. Oliver. Come in.

TRACY

(To Wallace.)
This is Ms. Morrison. She's one of our finest talent agents. I'm very proud of her.
(To Katie.)
This is Mr. Carris.

KATIE

Hello, nice to meet you, Mr. Carris. I believe we spoke on the phone.

WALLACE

Yes, I remember now. Pleasure to finally meet you.

TRACY

(She hands Katie the portfolio.)
Now that you two have officially met, I'll leave you alone to work out the business details. I'll be back in a few minutes to see about a possible contract.
(Tracy exits.)

KATIE

(She glances over the portfolio.)
Now, Mr. Carris...

WALLACE

(He smiles and holds out his hand.)
Please, call me Wallace.

KATIE

(She shakes his hand and then motions for Wallace to sit. He does so, gently setting his briefcase on the floor beside his chair.)
I see that your client, Mr. Hyde, came highly recommended to us. His record and past stage experience is impressive. He's almost too qualified for what we need.

WALLACE

(With growing excitement in his voice.)
Hopefully you won't leave him out in the cold over a simple thing such as over qualification. My client has specifically stated in his cover letter to this business that he is willing to take a pay cut for this job.
(He stands.)
He is most interested in performing for *this* audience! It's been his dream!

KATIE

I didn't realize that Mr. Hyde had such an affinity for our clientele.

WALLACE

Oh, he loves such audiences. He craves such audiences. They are his favorites!

KATIE

All right. But does Mr. Hyde realize the maturity level of this business' clientele? It says here he's been performing professionally for years. His material may not be appreciated.

WALLACE

Pshaw!
   (He sits.)
He's ready for a change. And that's why he sent me here to you fine people! To this fine establishment!

KATIE

As, um, excited as we are to hear this… the question is, why now?

WALLACE

Hmmm. I don't really know the answer to that one.
   (Beat.)
Why don't we ask him now!

KATIE

We have a policy against phone interviews.

WALLACE

Oh, don't worry about that. He's here. We can ask the source.

KATIE

   (Looking at the door.)
Is he coming in right now? Where is he?
   (Wallace, using Katie's distraction with the door, opens his briefcase, pulls out a puppet and sets it on his hand.)

WALLACE

Ta-da! I present to you, Mr. Hyde!

KATIE

That's Mr. Hyde?
(Pause.)
Thank you for coming, Wallace.

WALLACE

(The puppet and Wallace 'look' at each other. He then manipulates the puppet to 'hide' its face on his shoulder.)
No! Wait! I apologize for my client. He's very shy. But, if you don't mind me saying, I think you just insulted him. Mr. Hyde doesn't take too kindly to criticism.

KATIE

But…

WALLACE

(Mr. Hyde looks at Katie and then turns back to Wallace and whispers in his ear. He laughs.)
Yes. I agree.
(Turning to Katie.)
Mr. Hyde says that he's sorry for deceiving you and that he hopes to change your mind about him. He thinks you're very beautiful and that blue is definitely your color.
(Mr. Hyde whispers again in his ear.)
It brings out your eyes.

KATIE

(Embarrassed.)
Oh, well thank you…
(Suddenly remembering that Mr. Hyde is a puppet.)
But, no, I'm sorry. I'm just not sure if Mr. Hyde is what we're looking for.
(She stands and gestures toward the door.)
…but thank you for coming in.
(Mr. Hyde whispers into Wallace's ear.)

WALLACE

Mr. Hyde wants to know why you're being so critical of him when he's been nothing but nice to you. I must admit, I'm curious myself.

KATIE

Mr. Carris…

WALLACE

Please, Ms. Morrison, as I said before, call me Wallace.

KATIE

Wallace. I'm sorry, but we just don't have room for Mr. Hyde. He's not…

WALLACE

Not what? Not classy enough? Not funny enough? What? He can work on it. He can improve.
   (Mr. Hyde nods his head in agreement.)

KATIE

He's not real.
   (Wallace and Mr. Hyde gasp.)

WALLACE

I must say, Ms. Morrison, we've heard insults before, but this very well crosses the line!

KATIE

But…

WALLACE

Shhhh!
   (Listening to Mr. Hyde.)
All right, I'll tell her. Ms. Morrison, he thinks you're being biased.

KATIE

Well, please tell Mr. Hyde that we don't have any openings for someone of your client's caliber. Try Sesame Street. Perhaps they have some openings.
   (Mr. Hyde whispers into Wallace's ear.)

WALLACE

Yes, I agree! Ms. Morrison, this is the last straw! This violates the equal employment opportunity law!
   (Leans into Mr. Hyde.)
He doesn't wish to do this, but you leave him no choice. My client has decided to sue.

KATIE

Oh! Now I've heard it all! Mr. Hyde is going to sue?

WALLACE

Yes, you heard correctly. My client is going to sue.

KATIE

Mr. Carris, I'm sorry. I can no longer tolerate this shenanigan! Mr. Hyde is not a living, breathing human! He's made of cloth! He's a puppet! Puppets can't sue!

WALLACE

We take offense to that!

KATIE

Fine! You wanna play that way?
   (She takes off her right shoe and sock. She places the sock on her right hand.)
Here's *my* legal representative, Mr. Jekyll!
   (She makes her sock puppet 'whisper' in her ear.)
Mr. Jekyll says that there are no legal grounds on which to sue me.

WALLACE

You can't fool us! That is not your legal repr... repre... that's not your lawyer! You're crazy! That's a sock!

(Katie picks up a marker and draws eyes and a mouth on the sock. There is a moment of tense silence while she draws. She then presents her sock puppet to Wallace.)

KATIE

There! Satisfied? As if you have room to talk! You're an agent to *The Muppet Show* reject!

WALLACE

(Pointing to Mr. Jekyll.)
If it were real, it'd have arms!

KATIE

I'll have you know, Kermit "The Frog" started as a sock!

WALLACE

Did Kermit have a hole in his head, too? Or was he from the "reinforced-toe" family?

KATIE

This hole? This hole is for you to guess which finger I'm holding up at you right now!
(She pokes her middle finger out through the hole in the sock.)

WALLACE

What are your lawyer's qualifications, huh? Inspected by number sixteen? The "Hanes Her Way" School of Law?

KATIE

(Mr. Jekyll rips off Mr. Hyde's toupee.)
We could tell that was a rug when he first walked in here!
(Mr. Hyde buries his head in Wallace's shoulder.)

WALLACE

(Wallace snatches back the toupee with his bare hand, throws down the toupee and covers Mr. Hyde's ears.)

You're only adding to the psychological damages. We're going to sue you and your company for all you're worth!

KATIE

(Manipulating the sock puppet.)
Mr. Jekyll says,…
(With great emphasis.)
…"bring it on!"
(Mr. Hyde and Mr. Jekyll start to fight as Katie and Wallace trade insults.)

WALLACE

My client came here for a job interview, not to wrangle with this law-school drop out with sagging elastic and reeking of athlete's foot!

KATIE

My attorney wants to know if your client was dressed by "blind eye for the puppet guy"!

WALLACE

Oh yeah?!

KATIE

Yeah!

WALLACE

Well, my client refuses to work for some half-rigged business whose employees take legal advice from a lawyer whose greatest case was Corns versus Bunions!

KATIE

Aarrrgh!
(Katie grabs Wallace, landing him face up across the desk. She strangles him with the sock puppet still on her hand. Mr. Hyde attempts first to pull Katie off and then begins to 'yell' for help. Katie then turns her attentions toward Mr. Hyde, pulling him off of Wallace's hand. She then grabs a pair of scissors and holds Wallace at bay by threatening to cut off Mr. Hyde's nose.)
One more move and Mr. Hyde gets it!

WALLACE

(Wallace backs away. Trying to calm Katie down.)
Aren't you in enough legal trouble as it is? Don't add homicide to the list!

KATIE

Take it back. Take... it... back!

WALLACE

Okay, I... no, *we* take it back!

KATIE

I want to talk to my lawyer.

WALLACE

(Attempting to reason with her.)
All right... but how can you talk to your attorney when he's biting my client's neck?
(Wallace and Katie simultaneously look at Mr. Hyde and Mr. Jekyll. They then look back at each other.)
If you and your legal counsel release my client, we'll leave and forget this ever happened.

KATIE

It's not that easy. Do you realize that in these last few moments, you've basically ruined my career?

WALLACE

It doesn't have to be this way.

KATIE

You leave me no choice.
(She raises the scissors again towards Mr. Hyde.)

WALLACE

No! Anything but that!

(In the middle of Katie's outburst, Tracy enters.)

TRACY

Katie! What do you think you're doing?!
(Katie looks up at Tracy and quickly places Mr. Hyde and the scissors behind her back. As Katie is defending herself, Wallace grabs Mr. Hyde and holds him close. He strokes the puppet's head and mouths "Are you okay? I'll never let go again." Tracy is oblivious to his actions; she concentrates fully on Katie.)

KATIE

Ms. Oliver! I'm terribly sorry about the commotion. This man's client is not what we're looking for, but he refuses to leave.

WALLACE

(Looking up at Tracy, he gently places Mr. Hyde on the chair.)
My client has done nothing but shower Ms. Morrison with compliments and yet she insists upon heaping insult after insult on him. She's even gone so far as to mock both my client and myself with crude gestures.
(He points to the sock puppet on Katie's hand and the scissors in the other. Katie drops the scissors and rips the sock off her hand, trying to hide it.)
As you can see, due to such actions, my client has no choice but to sue.

TRACY

Ms. Morrison, we've had a discussion about this before. If you keep insisting upon offending potential clients, you leave me with no choice but to let you go!

KATIE

But Ms. Oliver… this gentleman is a loon! He's representing a puppet!

TRACY

(To Wallace.)
Excuse me?!

WALLACE

I assure you, madam, my client is nothing of the sort. He is a talented, clever, high-class entertainer. He has had nothing but high reviews and recommendations.
(He hands Tracy a resume.)
Here's his resume.

TRACY

(She quickly looks over the resume.)
Everything seems to check out, Mr. Carris...

WALLACE

(He smiles and holds out his hand.)
Please, call me Wallace.

TRACY

Wallace, I am deeply sorry for my employee's behavior towards your client. He is *more* than qualified for the job, and I see no reason why Ms. Morrison would not hire him. Before he sues, I ask that your client reconsider his options. He is more than welcome to the job, if he wants it. I'm sure he will find it worth his while.
(Turns to Katie.)
As for you, Ms. Morrison, I'd like to have a word with you in my office.

KATIE

But... but...

TRACY

Now!
(Tracy exits. Katie follows, but throws a mean look at Wallace, who then places Mr. Hyde back on his hand.)

WALLACE

Did you hear that? You're hired!
(Hugs the puppet. Then listens to Mr. Hyde.)
Why you little ingrate! After what I just went through for you?
(Listens again. Shocked at what he hears.)

You can't fire me!

(He body-slams the puppet against the top of the desk. His hand is still inside the puppet. With his free hand, he grabs the scissors and raises them high in the air above the puppet.)

...'cause I quit!

(He plunges the scissors into the puppet and his own hand. He screams with pain as he realizes what he has done.)

AUGH!!

(Fast blackout as the curtain falls.)

BLACKOUT

Exhibit 4

*by Jeremy Kerr
and Amanda Miller*

Exhibit 4

*by Jeremy Kerr
and Amanda Miller*

THE CHARACTERS

A Man—Middle aged; oddly dressed.
Paul—Late twenties; handsome, but not terribly so. He wears slacks and a nice sweater.
Andrea—An attractive female in her late twenties. She is fashionably dressed, but casual.
A Guy—An average guy in his late twenties.

THE SCENE

The Setting: The large hallway of a famous art museum.
The Time: The present.

(Lights up to reveal the large hallway of an art museum. There is a large crate onstage, turned sideways. There appears to be a small access lid on the top side. Stenciled on the side of the crate are the words "Do Not Incinerate!" An oddly dressed MAN loiters next to the crate. After a few seconds, he speaks.)

MAN

Hot dogs! Red hot wieners! Get your hot dogs!
(Pause. He examines his fingernails. He is bored, but continues.)
Get 'em here! The hot dogs. You can get 'em… here.
(He trails off.)
Get 'em.
(PAUL and ANDREA enter from right. Paul is reading from a brochure.)

PAUL

Exhibit Four is Monet's "Water Lilies."

ANDREA

No, it's not.

Exhibit 4   17

PAUL

(Still looking at brochure.)
Yes, it is. Listen to this: "Exhibit Four, French Impressionist Claude Monet's *Water Lilies*."

ANDREA

Well, if it is, they forgot to unpack it.

PAUL

(Looking up.)
Oh! Oh, wow. Now that's odd.

MAN

Hot dogs!

PAUL

Pardon me, sir. Could you tell me where we might find Exhibit Four?

MAN

Red hots!

PAUL

Oh.

ANDREA

Maybe we should just go on to Exhibit Five, Paul.

PAUL

What? No. I'm sure there's some reason for this, Andrea.
(To the man.)
Do you work for the museum?

MAN

Hot dogs.

ANDREA

Maybe they replaced Monet with some performance art. I hear that's all the rage in New York right now.

PAUL

Yeah, maybe so.

MAN

Foot longs!

ANDREA

So, we should stay and watch. He might do something—

MAN

(Interrupting.)
Mustard! Relish!
(Sighs.)
Hot dogs.

PAUL

Fascinating.

ANDREA

Yeah.

MAN

Hot dogs. They're here. You want 'em; I got 'em.

PAUL

So, where were you last night?

ANDREA

Why?

Exhibit 4   19

PAUL

You said you'd call. You never did.

ANDREA

I was busy.

PAUL

Fine.

MAN

Hot dogs!

ANDREA

Exhibit Three was cool.

PAUL

Yeah.

ANDREA

You know what else was cool?

MAN

Hot dogs.
  (They laugh.)

PAUL

Yeah, hot dogs are cool.

MAN

Foot longs!
  (The box shakes from inside.)

BOTH

Oooooo!

ANDREA

Now *that* was cool.

PAUL

Yep.
    (Beat.)
So who were you with?

ANDREA

Paul!?

PAUL

What? I think it's a fair question.

MAN

Hot dogs!

ANDREA

I was with "hot dogs." Alright?!

PAUL

Whatever.

MAN

Hot dogs!
    (Box shakes again.)

ANDREA

So, what do you think is in the crate?

PAUL

A person.

ANDREA

Real creative.

Exhibit 4 21

PAUL

What? We're in a museum watching performance art. What else would it be? They aren't going to put a load of badgers in a crate.

ANDREA

Now that's a creative answer... badgers! Of course it's a person... I just meant... what do you think is supposed to be inside for the show? I think it's hot dogs.

PAUL

Wouldn't that be a bit obvious? He's standing there yelling "hot dogs."

MAN

Hot dogs!

PAUL

Obvious.

MAN

Red hots!

ANDREA

I was with Lewis! You happy now?

PAUL

Lewis?!

MAN

Hot dogs!

PAUL

What were you doing with Lewis?

ANDREA

Maybe we were eating hot dogs!

                         MAN

Hot dogs!

                         PAUL

Hot dogs?!

                       ANDREA

Or maybe we were eating pizza and then hanging out at the coffee shop!

                         PAUL

Coffee shop?!

                         MAN

Hot dogs!

                       ANDREA

And pizza!

                         PAUL

So was it a date?

                       ANDREA

Yes.

                         PAUL

I thought *we* were dating.

                       ANDREA

You thought wrong.

                         PAUL

But we always go out.

                       ANDREA

…as friends.

Exhibit 4   23

PAUL

But I really like you, Andrea.

ANDREA

I know, Paul. And I like you, too… but just as friends. I thought you understood that.

PAUL

How would I have known that?

ANDREA

Because we talked about it last week. Same conversation, different venue.

PAUL

Well… yeah… but… Since then, I thought—

MAN

Foot longs!

ANDREA

No, Paul.

PAUL

Oh… I see.
    (Box shakes.)

ANDREA

So, what do you think is in the crate?

PAUL

    (Mumbles.)
Badgers.

ANDREA

You already used badgers.

PAUL

Then... I don't know... Squirrels?

ANDREA

Does it have to be a rodent?

PAUL

Does it have to be Lewis?

ANDREA

In the box?

PAUL

No. That you're dating. He's my roommate. Why would you choose to date my roommate when you know *I* like you? Hello, Hurtful!

ANDREA

Paul—

MAN

Hot dogs!

ANDREA

(To man.)
Shut up!

PAUL

You can't yell at him. What are you doing?

ANDREA

Why can't I?

PAUL

Because he's "Art."

Exhibit 4   25

ANDREA

Art? Whatever. He's yelling "hot dogs!"

MAN

Foot longs!

PAUL

And red hots... but so what? Who are you to say what art is or isn't?
  (Box shakes.)

ANDREA

  (Referring to shaking.)
And what's with that?

PAUL

Look, we can go on to Exhibit Five, if you want.

ANDREA

He kissed *me*, okay?

PAUL

What?

ANDREA

Lewis. *He* kissed *me*. We were hanging out as friends and one day he kissed me. I realized I really liked him and we started dating.

PAUL

When did he kiss you?

MAN

Hot dogs!

ANDREA

Tuesday.

PAUL

It's only Saturday. In four days the two of you have become "an item?"

ANDREA

Yes.

PAUL

So if I had kissed you last week at the museum, we'd be dating?

MAN

Ketchup.

ANDREA

No.

PAUL

Why not?

ANDREA

Because last week we were discussing how I didn't like you that way.

MAN

Foot longs!

PAUL

(To the man.)
Shut up!

ANDREA

You can't yell at him.

PAUL

Why not? It's not "Art," remember?

Exhibit 4   27

ANDREA

Because you told me I couldn't yell at him.

MAN

Hot dogs!

BOTH

Shut up!

ANDREA

This is ridiculous. Why don't we go home?

PAUL

Don't you want to see Exhibit Five?

ANDREA

Not really, no.
  (Box shakes.)

PAUL

Don't you want to see what's in the crate?

ANDREA

A person, Paul. A person is in the crate. Don't be an idiot.

PAUL

I just meant... you know... the performance piece.

ANDREA

Forget it. Who cares? It's a stupid show anyway. Let's just go.

PAUL

Okay, whatever.

MAN

Hot dogs! Foot longs!
   (As they exit right, they pass A GUY. He walks to the Hot Dog Man.)

A GUY

   (To the Hot Dog Man.)
I'll take one.
   (Hot Dog Man opens the crate and gets out a hot dog.)

MAN

That'll be three-fifty.

A GUY

Thanks.
   (There is an exchange of money and the guy exits off left eating his hot dog.)

MAN

Red hots! Foot longs!
   (The lights begin to fade.)

BLACKOUT

The Doctor is Out

by Meg Elliot
with Tiffany Stephens

The Doctor is Out

by Meg Elliott
with Tiffany Stephens

THE CHARACTERS

Connie—A mild-mannered psychiatrist in her mid thirties. She wears glasses.
Roger—A troubled young man in his mid-twenties with an attitude.

THE SCENE

The Setting: The medical practice of Dr. Connie Johnson, Psychiatrist.
The Time: The present.

(At lights up, we see CONNIE sitting in her rocking chair with her eyes closed and a notepad on her lap. Connie's office is lightly furnished with a desk and chair, a rocking chair, and a psychiatrist's couch. There is a knocking sound offstage.)

CONNIE

(Waking with a start.)
Oh, come in, please.
(Enter ROGER. He has a look of annoyance and boredom on his face.)
Hello. I'm Dr. Johnson, but you can call me Connie.
(Holds out her hand. Roger grudgingly and briefly shakes it.)
I take it you're Roger.

ROGER

Yeah, yeah. Let's just get this over with.

CONNIE

Very well. Please, take a seat.
(She indicates that he should sit on the couch; he does. She crosses and sits in the rocker. Nervously, he shifts his positions; he first throws one leg over the couch, then lays down on his belly, and then sits up straight. She adjusts her notepad and settles into the chair.)
Now, Roger…
(He is bouncing on the couch, oblivious to her.)
Roger? Roger!

ROGER

Hmm? What?!

CONNIE

Roger, do you know why you're here?

ROGER

Yeah, some punk at the movie theater was blocking my view, so I punched his lights out, and there was a cop sitting behind me that saw the whole thing. Big deal.

CONNIE

It *is* a big deal, Roger.

ROGER

Why?

CONNIE

Because then you hit the cop.

ROGER

Yeah, yeah. So now this judge tells me I either gotta spend twenty-five hours talking to you or spend the next six months in jail.

CONNIE

Well, clearly you have an aggression problem and you need help.

ROGER

Look, I'm sure you got something you'd rather do than sit here and listen to me talk about my "troubled childhood" and my "social difficulties." So why don't you do us both a favor—sign my papers and make us both happier, huh?

CONNIE

You know I can't do that, Roger. So, please, just lie back and talk to me, okay? Now, where did you grow up?

ROGER

(Sighs.)
San Francisco.

CONNIE

Really? How interesting! I'm from the Bay Area, myself. Tell me about it.

ROGER

Oh, okay… Well, my dad left when I was about six, so it was just me and my mom. I guess you could say I was…
(He does air quotes with his fingers.)
…"deprived of a father figure" or something like that.
(Connie starts to drift off to sleep on the word "just." After a few seconds, she lets out a loud snore on the word "something.")
Hey! Hey, Doc?! Yo! Wake up!

CONNIE

(Awakes.)
Huh? What? Oh… Oh, my goodness, not again…

ROGER

What? What's your problem?

CONNIE

(Laughs nervously.)
Ha-ha, isn't that usually my line? Ha-ha…
(Sighs.)
Roger, I am so sorry. You see, I… I suffer from narcolepsy.

ROGER

What's that?

CONNIE

Well, it's an ailment that causes me to just spontaneously fall asleep. I'll be sitting there, wide awake, and then just sort of… conk out! Oh, it's just awful. I even fell asleep during my sister's wedding… But I am quite sure I am better now. Ahem … please, continue.

ROGER

You sure you're okay?

CONNIE

Quite, thank you. Now, you were saying…?

ROGER

Okay… so my mom's boyfriend took me to the park and everything was okay until this pigeon crapped on my head and it started running down my neck to my back.

(Connie drifts off to sleep on the word "everything." She shifts her position on the second word "and." She continues to shift in her chair, subtly at first, but begins to thrash around with sharp movements on the word "neck.")
Hey! *Hey!* Wake up!!

CONNIE

(She falls out of the rocking chair in a forward motion.)
Oh, Roger, I am sorry.
(He helps her up.)

ROGER

Look, Doc, obviously you have some kind of medical thing… so why don't you just sign my papers and I'll go… so you can get some pills or shock treatments… or a nap?

CONNIE

Roger, no… I have been entrusted with getting you better. I will not allow your treatment to be derailed by the mere fact that I fall asleep every few minutes. Please, sit back down and we will continue with the session. Now, where were we?

ROGER

A pigeon crapped in my hair.

CONNIE

Ah, yes. And how did that make you feel?

ROGER

Crappy.

CONNIE

Understandable.
(Makes notes on pad.)

ROGER

So anyways, my mom's boyfriend—big jerk—he starts laughing at me, right? Well, I wasn't gonna take anymore crap that day, especially not from him! So I punched him in the gut...
(He gets up to demonstrate; he really gets into it.)
I was like this...
(He swings.)
...and he was like that...
(He falls back, while Connie drifts off again on "So." She starts mumbling to herself on "I was like...".)

CONNIE

(She mumbles.)
Mmumbluuu.... Himminuhuu."
Oh, no! Not again, man! Yo, Doc! *Get up!*
(Connie mumbles.)
Mmm... why is all the rum gone?... mmm...
(Roger goes behind the rocking chair and shakes it back and forth rapidly.)
Aaaahhhh! Stop! Stop it!
(He does. She begins to adjust her hair and blouse.)
Oh, my goodness.

ROGER

You know, Doc, you really aren't much help to anyone if you're gonna fall asleep all the time.

CONNIE

(Clearly offended.)

Excuse me. *Who* is the doctor here? That's right, I am! And you, Mr. I-punched-some-punk-and-a-cop-cause-a-bird-crapped-on-my-head, are hardly in a position to tell someone that they need help! Now, I may be unable to maintain consciousness for extended periods of time, but I am still fully qualified to deal with delinquents such as yourself!

(Regains her composure.)

Now, please… continue.

ROGER

O-kay… So after I hit the guy, they sent me to Juvie for six months. And I won't lie…

(Big pause.)

… I was scared…

(Connie falls asleep yet again on "And" and begins snoring loudly, punctuating "scared" with a very loud snore.)

All right! That's it!

(Goes over to Connie and shakes her by the shoulders.)

Wake up!

CONNIE

Ouch! Hey! Hey! Do you want to add another count of assault to your repertoire, mister?

ROGER

No, but listen…! You are not helping me here. What good are you going to do me or anyone else with their problems, if you can barely stay awake to hear them? Now either find some way to keep from falling asleep or find me another doctor to "psychologize" me and sign my papers, so I can be done with my sentence!

CONNIE

(Utterly dejected.)

You're right, you know? How can I help anyone, if I can't even help myself? All this time I wanted to let people know that their problems don't define them and now I can't even solve my own problems!

(Her weeping builds up to a point where her words are indiscernible, "solve my own problems" sounds like "sahmahohnpahmas." She then begins crying loudly.)

ROGER

Hey. Hey, don't cry. I mean it. Stop crying! Now!
(On the word "Stop" he brings her over to the couch and sits her down. He sits next to her. She stops crying.)
Man! How long have you had this problem, anyway?

CONNIE

All my life. I can't remember ever being able to stay awake for a whole day. I almost did, once, in the fourth grade. I made it all the way to lunchtime, but then I fell asleep in my applesauce. It went up my nose... and I was sneezing out applesauce all day long and... well, I'm sure you can guess where my classmates went with that...
(She starts to slowly drift off again and her head leans to the side on the word "went." After "that" she is asleep on his shoulder.)

ROGER

(Not realizing she is on his shoulder yet.)
Ouch.
(Realizes she is out again. Rolls his eyes.)
Great.
(Raising his voice.)
Hey, Doc!
(He gets up and stands. She awakes with a start.)
Must be rough... falling asleep all the time.

CONNIE

Oh, it's awful. Just awful. I barely made it through grad school. I couldn't get through a single class without conking out and drowning out the professor's lecture with my snores. You know, it took me nine years to get my counseling license. And of course, my husband gets the worst of it. Why, I snore louder than he does! He's always saying, "Connie, I can't take you anywhere!"
(Starts to cry again.)

ROGER

Yes…
(Sits down in the rocking chair, leans back and puts his hands behind his head.)
And how does that make you feel?
(Connie continues talking and crying. She lies back on the couch.)
Well, it all started when I fell asleep at Thanksgiving dinner and fell face first into
Mother's candied yams and sent the rolls flying into the cranberry sauce.
*(While he listens, Roger slowly starts to fall asleep on the word "Thanksgiving." He
lets out a few soft but noticeable snores as she talks throughout. Lights begin to fade.)*

BLACKOUT

Good Help

by George Harrison Hendricks IV

Good Help

by George Harrison Hendricks IV

THE CHARACTERS

Dr. Karl von Werner—Mad scientist. Messily dressed. Lab coat. Typical geek couture. He could be quite handsome, if he'd clean up a bit.
Igor—Hunchback. Shabbily dressed. Greasy hair. He speaks with a thick Cockney accent.

THE SCENE

The Setting: The laboratory of Dr. Karl von Werner. The lab is full with electronic equipment and machinery reminiscent of a Bela Lugosi movie only with a high-tech twist.
The Time: The present.

(Lights up on IGOR typing sporadically but efficiently on a laptop computer. He wears oversized headphones. His expression reflects his serious endeavor. A round, red button glows conspicuously on the wall. Electronic bleeps and boops accompany his actions. Enter DR. KARL. Dressed in a white lab coat, he has a very intense look on his face.)

DR. KARL

Are we ready?

IGOR

Yeth, Mathter.

DR. KARL

EYE-gor—

IGOR

EE-gor, thir.

DR. KARL

EE-gor? Are you certain?

IGOR

Thinth the day I wath born, Mathter.

DR. KARL

Whatever.
  (Notices the bulge in Igor's cheek.)
I thought I told you, no candy in the laboratory.

IGOR

Thorry, Math…
  (Igor takes the jawbreaker out of his mouth and throws it in the trashcan.)
Sorry, Master. I'll forget me own head next.

DR. KARL

Never mind that. How are the preparations coming?

IGOR

Very well, Master, very well indeed.

DR. KARL

Have you integrated the new thrust vectors?

IGOR

I did that before lunch, Master.

DR. KARL

Recalibrated the ignition boosters to compensate for the high winds?

IGOR

I did that twice, just to be safe.

DR. KARL

  (Pauses for a moment to think of something else.)
Did you pick up my dry cleaning?

IGOR

It won't be ready until tomorrow.

DR. KARL

Oh, well. I should have liked to have worn my smoking jacket one last time.
(Thinks of something very funny. Proceeds with maniacal laughter.)
Not to worry. This time tomorrow we'll *all* be wearing smoking jackets!
(Continues laughing as he moves to downstage center for next speech. The stage lights dim slightly as a single spotlight draws focus to Dr. Karl.)
Excellent! We're so close. This is the moment of my destiny. Every breath I've ever taken has been for the sole purpose of propelling my body and mind to this point in time. At last, they will see my true genius unfold before their eyes in brilliant red-orange hues.
(A fiery glow from a spotlight overhead colors his face. Screams are heard in the distance during the remainder of the monologue.)
The children of the world will weep as they taste the coppery tang of fear moments before their lives and the lives of the mindless barbarians who spawned them are snuffed out in a sweet chorus of screams. The flickering lights of their lives extinguished like birthday candles in a hurricane! I shall become the right hand of God and the left hand of Satan as I rain down my righteous and unholy vengeance upon their fat cow heads! The world will perish! Vanish in a hail of fire and stone! I shall smite the human race into extinction, and the last expression to cross their heathen faces will be the realization that it was *I* who brought this down upon them!
(Igor looks up and realizes he's missed something important.)

IGOR

Brought what down? I'm sorry, Master. I wasn't listening. *Abba Gold*… captivates me every time.
(Starts singing Dancing Queen and moving his feet to the music. Dr. Karl's reaction brings Igor back to reality.)
You were saying something?

DR. KARL

(Looking bewildered and slightly hurt that his big speech went unnoticed.)
Oh. Ummmm… I was just saying that I… well, *we*… were going to rain unholy vengeance upon the unwashed masses.

IGOR

Unwashed masses, eh? Unholy vengeance, you say? And how are we going to go about that?

DR. KARL

(Completely taken aback.)
Awha? But… but… but… You're my… You've got… We've been… You work for me, don't you?

IGOR

Hmm? Oh, yes. And it's a lovely job. Good hours. Interesting work. And some of the best health coverage I've ever come across in my career as a henchman.

DR. KARL

(Caught off guard by the compliment.)
Oh, well, yes. I always say, "Take care of your employees and they'll take care of you."

IGOR

That is so true. That is so true. Just the other day I was telling my dear old Dad that… Well, bugger that for a lark, it's completely left my head, it has. No bother. I'm sure it was complimentary.

DR. KARL

Yes, well, I'm sure it was, but we were discussing your employment here.

IGOR

Oh, yes. And it's a lovely job. Good hours. Interesting work. And some of the best health coverage…

DR. KARL

Yes, thank you, Igor. I'm very aware of your appreciation for the benefits package, but—

IGOR

Too right I appreciate it! With a body like mine you aren't exactly rolling around in the green, grassy meadows of good health, if you catch my meaning. Why, the osteopath bills alone would be enough to put me in debtor's prison. It's a wonder—

DR. KARL

Silence!

IGOR

Oh, all right. You don't have to go yelling about it. I'll be quiet if you want me to. "No use going on and on for no real reason," my dear old Dad would say. Why, just the other day he...
(Sees the Doctor's expression.)
Shutting up now, Master.

DR. KARL

(Composing himself.)
Let's try a different approach. How long have you been working for me?

IGOR

Let me think for a moment.
(He looks at the ceiling. Proceeds to think. And think. And think. And think.)

DR. KARL

(Impatient.)
Well?

IGOR

Did you know... that ceiling tile right there has a water spot in it that looks like Elvis? Costello not Presley. I've been a roadie for both, and let me tell you—"The King" is no royalty. Table manners of a four-year-old, he has. I do need a picture of this.
(Gets up to get his camera.)
Me mum will go wild. Swears she once threw her knickers at Mr. Presley when he came through—

DR. KARL

(Yelling.)
How long have you been working here?!

IGOR

Well, there you go yelling again. Remember your cholesterol… and your ulcers. Getting worked up like that ain't good for either of them, if you don't mind me saying so. Why not have a sit and I'll fix you a nice cup of tea. Doesn't that sound lovely? Let me go put the—

DR. KARL

How long!

IGOR

Oh, that. Three years next Tuesday. I started on a Tuesday on account of Monday being a holiday and all. Shall I put the kettle on?

DR. KARL

(Quite pleasant now that he's gotten his answer.)
Yes, please. That *would* be lovely.
(Realization hits.)
Three years?! Three years? Three?

IGOR

(Distracted with the tea pot.)
Hmm? Oh, yes, right after your wife left, if I recall correctly.

DR. KARL

Three years and you have no idea what we're doing and what we're trying to accomplish… and I thought I told you to never mention her name in this laboratory… *ever!*

IGOR

I did no such thing. I said, "your wife." I did not say, "Judith"—

DR. KARL

Never!

IGOR

I was only trying to illustrate how I hadn't actually said, "Judith"—
   (Dr. Karl gives Igor a warning finger.)
All right, all right. I can take a hint. You don't have to tell me twice.
   (Long pause.)
She really is a lovely woman though. I saw her just last week at the market when I went in to pick up your blood-pressure medicine. She asked about you.

DR. KARL

I *said*…
   (It hits him what Igor has said.)
She did? What did she say?

IGOR

Oh, nothing really. She just asked how you were getting on, if you were keeping up with your diet. That sort of thing. Oh! She showed me pictures of the new baby, and my goodness wasn't it just precious.
   (Slips into mommy-speak.)
Those widdle pink toeses and it's adorable widdle fingers, and a full head of…
   (Igor realizes that it's exceptionally quiet—the kind of quiet that's so loud you can't hear yourself think.)
…to tell you the truth, it's an ugly thing. Looked somewhat like a bulldog in a bonnet. Had to bite my lip to keep my lunch down. Triggered my fight or flight response it almost did. Good thing it wasn't there with her. I might have started throwing cans of corn at it until it scuttled off into the frozen foods. Hideous child.
   (Realizes this isn't helping much.)
So, what is it we do around here again? I seem to recall that being the crux of the conversation and, to be honest, I have always been a bit curious. Just never thought to ask. All these knobs and gizmos and you hammering away and such into all hours of the night—

DR. KARL

(Startled by the change in topic.)
You've been involved in every phase of the project for *three* years, and you're just now getting around to asking what it is we're doing?

IGOR

Oh, I've never been one for the big picture. I'm more of a detail man myself. "Can't see the forest for the trees," my dear old Dad always says. Give me a job to do and I'll get it done or Bob's your Uncle. Don't go around asking questions though. It's above my station.

DR. KARL

(With great impatience at Igor's lack of vision.)
We're going to launch a rocket at the moon! A rocket tipped with a solid diamond drill which *you* designed.

IGOR

That wasn't for the garden?

DR. KARL

(Getting worked up.)
Upon impact, it will bore its way to the center of the moon. Once there, it will detonate a 1,000-megaton nuclear device, splitting the moon like a ripe watermelon.

IGOR

Oh, I like watermelon.

DR. KARL

The fragments of the once majestic celestial body will get sucked down by the earth's powerful gravitational field, hurtling continent-sized chunks of rock into the earth's atmosphere. Whatever isn't killed by the initial impact will soon succumb to the earthquakes, tsunami, and resultant ice age! The destruction will be beautiful and complete. It will—

IGOR

Well, what do you want to go and do a thing like that for?

DR. KARL

(Taken aback.)
Well… because I can.

IGOR

I can put on a tiara and go around calling myself the Queen Mum, but that don't mean it's meant to be done, now does it?

DR. KARL

But you see, the earth is teeming with the filthy, dirty disease called Man. Humanity doesn't deserve to see another sunrise.

IGOR

That may be so… that may be so. Many of them don't… but that doesn't mean you should be the one to make that decision for them. Who do you think you are? Oh, wait just a minute… I think I know what's going on here.

DR. KARL

Yes, as do I. We're going to destroy the planet with a push of that flashing red button over there.

IGOR

What for? Were you picked on as a child? Did your mummy love you too much? …or not enough? …walk in on your dad trying on your mum's knickers? They never buy you that puppy you're always going on about in your sleep?

DR. KARL

What?! No! That's preposterous. A complete fabrication. You should get a job with the BBC.
(Long, uncomfortable pause. He sags into a chair.)
How in bloody blazes do you know all of that?

IGOR

You're a textbook case of base megalomania coupled with, and fueled by, classic narcissistic rage. You were a sickly child I'd wager. Mummy never really cut the apron strings?

DR. KARL

How do you know all this? I thought you never paid attention to details?

IGOR

When it comes to diabolical master plans? No. Can't be bothered. I'm more of a people person. Besides, you're not the first mad scientist I've worked for. I spent a few years digging up bits and pieces for a nice gent who helped put God Complex on the map, which you also exhibit signs of, if you don't mind me saying. Anyway, you can't go juggling heads for a living without learning a thing or two about their insides. But my work history isn't the issue here, it's you and your over-developed sense of entitlement that's got us in a bit of a quandary.

DR. KARL

Ohhh, I beg to differ! I'm doing this for far nobler reasons than mere psychological scarring. Mummy's knickers don't even play into it!
  (He pauses... thinks... lets out a small whimper... catches himself... continues.)
I do this for every baby born addicted to crack; every malnourished child doomed to an early grave by a greedy government; for every poor chap who's walked in on his two-timing whore-of-a-wife shagging the butcher on the Italian leather sofa you purchased for your fifteenth wedding anniversary!

IGOR

You didn't even pay retail for it, but go ahead and blame it on her and the furniture if you want to. Blame it on everyone but yourself. You know full well that your marriage was dead long before she started snogging the local meat-cutter. No, no, no, no! ... I know what's going on here.

DR. KARL

Oh, do tell.

IGOR

All of this revolves around your... ahem... "problem" and the source of your problem.

DR. KARL

Problem?

IGOR

Yes. "Problem."

DR. KARL

And what, pray tell, might that be?
(Igor holds up his fist and shakes it a bit. Then lets it droop ninety degrees. Dr. Karl plays dumb. Igor does it again, but accompanies the droop with a sound effect. Dr. Karl's eyes go wide.)

DR. KARL

What?! I don't have a problem with that! My "special place" is just as effective as it's always been.

IGOR

Do you think your marriage ended because of your problem, or your problem... ahem... "popped up" because your marriage was in trouble? I've been chicken and egging it in my head for years now. I can only imagine how it's been bugging you all those long, lonely nights in the labora—

DR. KARL

No! No problem. None. Zero. Not a blessed bit! I'm strong like a bull! I'm beastly and virile. Why just this last weekend I bedded two... no, three lovely young ladies in quick succession! At the same time even!
(Igor listens to the sad, pathetic, and obviously false rant. Shaking his head all the while.)

IGOR

Really? What were their names?

DR. KARL

Oh… I… didn't bother to learn their names! I wasn't planning on sending them birthday cards.
(Winking with nudging gestures.)

IGOR

Ohhh, look at the big, bad sex machine. Do you come with a warning label? "Caution! Contents may produce hot, hot heat!" That makes you a man, does it? That shows the world you've got it all together? Come off it, Master. You and I both know where you were this weekend. You were in a holly bush outside Judith's bedroom window with a pair of field glasses. That woman hasn't left your thoughts a single day since she left you. She's the impetus for all this.

DR. KARL

Impetus! Nonsense! I'm *not* impot…

IGOR

Oh, come now! You're attempting to destroy the planet with a rocket. Need I outline the various Freudian elements involved in this plan? You can't let her go. You feel that her leaving you was the end of your world, so you decided to end everyone else's. I've got two words for you: "Grow. Up." You could have actually bedded those three young ladies you alluded to, if you'd let the past die and step into the present. You don't need to carry on like this.

DR. KARL

I'm not carrying on!
(He walks over to the button with grim determination. The next lines are delivered with almost manic desperation.)
I'm doing this for the little guy; every single mother forced to work three jobs so she and her child can slip further into poverty; every victim of a school bully who'd rather bring a gun to school than take another beating; every ignorant farmer getting paid by the government *not* to grow corn—

IGOR

(Igor gets angry. As he continues, he gets angrier, and as he gets angrier, he begins to stand taller.)

Every time you rationalize your actions, you slip farther away from the humanity you're supposedly helping. I bet if you went outside for once and actually asked the wretched masses if they'd appreciate being relieved of their lives, you'd see that most of them wouldn't take too well to the idea. You're not God. You're not Shiva. You're not a great crusader for the downtrodden. You're not even a very good scientist. You're not anything but a selfish, petty little man who needs to get laid! Now step away from that button before you see a firsthand demonstration of what happens when diplomacy fails!

(He cracks his knuckles. Dr. Karl pauses, considers his actions, and then collapses on the floor in tears.)

DR. KARL

Oh, my sweet, baby Jesus! Igor... What have I become?

IGOR

There, there, you've not become anything yet. You can still change... and I'll do my best to help.

DR. KARL

I really did love her... once.

IGOR

And I know she feels the same way.

DR. KARL

(Extremely emotional. Almost in tears.)
Thank you, Igor. Thank you so much.

IGOR

It's no bother.
(Helps Dr. Karl to his feet.)
Now, how about that cup of tea? I got a fresh tin of biscuits at the market last week. Jammy Dodgers. Your favorite.
(Dr. Karl manages a weak smile.)

DR. KARL

That sounds wonderful.

(He crosses to the kettle. Igor goes over to the laptop, studies the screen for a moment, and then presses a button. The flashing red light goes out. Igor shakes his head and then closes the laptop.)

IGOR

I take mine with milk and sugar, Master.

(Dr. Karl does a double-take over his shoulder as the lights fade.)

BLACKOUT

Paper Football

by Brad Archer
with Meg Elliot

Paper Football

by Brad Archer
with Meg Elliot

THE CHARACTERS

Chad—Male; mid twenties. A normal guy, but not too bright.
Sam—Female; mid twenties. Attractive, but a bit shy.
Dick—Male; early twenties. Handsome in a weird sort of way.
Barbie & Judy—Two attractive, athletic-looking joggers in their early twenties.

THE SCENE

The Setting: A bench in the park.
The Time: The present.

(At lights up, we see CHAD and SAM sitting on a park bench cuddling. Chad whispers sweet nothings in her ear; Sam giggles like a little school girl. The tranquility of the moment is interrupted suddenly as DICK enters howling obnoxiously. He wears and carries a slew of Kansas City Chiefs fan paraphernalia, including a large Arrowhead foam hat, a large foam finger, several pennants, and various "football foods." He has a football ticket in his pocket.)

DICK

Whooooooo!! Oh yeah!!
(Chad and Sam stare at the lumbering figure of the over-spirited Dick, who continues to "whoop it up." As he approaches their bench, Dick looks first at his ticket and then at the bench, and then back to the ticket. After a short moment, Dick squeezes between the two lovebirds.)

CHAD

(Chad stands.)
Whoa! Look here, buddy, what are you doing?

DICK

Oh, I got "Row A, Seat Number Two," and that'd be right here. See?
(Pointing to the seating positions on the bench.)
Seat one, two, and three.

(On "one" he points at the empty seat on his left. On "two" he points to his own seat. On "three" he points to the seat where Sam is seated, but places his hand on her knee in the process. Sam reacts with surprise, brushing his hand aside.)

CHAD

(Pointing at the ticket.)
What is that?

DICK

A ticket for the game.
(Dick suddenly shouts, bursting with random excitement for the pending game.)
YEAH!!

CHAD

What are you doing?

DICK

(Spelling it out.)
I came to watch the game. This is my ticket. This is my seat. Okay? Good.

CHAD

Game? What game?

DICK

Der! The CNAA Finals. The national championship. The ultimate showdown!

CHAD

CNAA?

DICK

CNAA.
(No response from Chad.)
Collegiate NON-Athletic Association.

SAM

Non-athletic sports?

DICK

Yeah, ya' know, like, underwater basket weaving, ultimate hangman, turkey hunting, NASCAR... that kind of stuff. My roommate is the captain of the paper football team.

CHAD

Look at what you're wearing! The Kansas City Chiefs aren't even a college team!

DICK

Shhh! Here come the cheerleaders!
 (Two attractive female joggers run by.)

CHAD

 (Looking at Sam who remains speechless.)
This is insane!

DICK

I know! They didn't even dance! ... I mean, you pay... like, what... fifty bucks to even get into the stadium... it'd be nice to have a little more action than that, you know?

CHAD

Fifty bucks? What are you talking about?

DICK

Whoa, you didn't pay to get in here?
 (Pause.)
Damn it! Are you freakin kidding me? That son of a—
 (Beat.)
...ripped me off! Probably used it to buy crack!

CHAD

What? Is this a joke?!

DICK

Hey! … They're coming back!
(Female joggers return, stopping to stretch.)
Oh! There they go!
(He whistles as they stretch.)
Yeah!! I paid 50 bucks, but for this… I'd have paid 100, baby!
(He continues to whistle and cheer.)
Hey, Baby! That's my girl!
(The girls, disgusted and a little frightened, continue on their way.)
Hey, whoa! Where you going?
(To Sam.)
Psshh. Divas! Can't even take a compliment.

CHAD

Okay, look. Can we just switch seats? I came here to be with my girlfriend.

DICK

Look, dude! It isn't my fault you didn't reserve the seat *next* to you for your woman.

CHAD

How can you reserve a park bench?!

DICK

I did. Says it r*ight here.*
(Pointing to the ticket. Chad inspects the ticket.)

CHAD

That looks like you wrote it by hand!

SAM

Chad, just leave him alone. Let him watch his game.

DICK

(Dick struggles to eat his hot dog because of all the cumbersome props he brought with him.)

Hey, can you hold this?
(*Shoves the fan junk into Chad's hands.*)

SAM

(*Standing.*)
Chad?
(*Sweetly.*)
Let's just go somewhere else… Okay?

CHAD

No! I came to the park to have a nice time with you and that's what I'm going to do!
(*Slams the junk down.*)

DICK

(*He gasps.*)
How dare you defile the sacred "Paper-Football-Game-Watching Survival Kit!!"

CHAD

The what?

DICK

(*Upset that Chad has offended the gods. Sam sits back down.*)
You must repent… or the wrath of the almighty paper football gods will surely annihilate you!

CHAD

Paper football gods?

DICK

(*Chanting in a strange tongue. He stomps and dances a ritual dance as he chants.*)
Unga, mocha, kringle, shoob! Unga, mocha, kringle, shoob! Unga, mocha, kringle, shoob! Unga—

CHAD

What are you doing?

DICK

(*Continues to chant and begins dancing in circles.*)
Do it with me! Unga, mocha, kringle, shoob!

CHAD

No, I will not!

SAM

(*Beginning to feel pity for the psycho.*)
Chad, just do what he says...

DICK

Yes, Chad. By ignoring the rituals, you only anger the gods more!

CHAD

But—

DICK

Hurry! Time is a factor that must not be ignored!

CHAD

Fine!

DICK

Follow me, now.
    (*He stomps as he speaks. Chad imitates his moves.*)
Unga!

CHAD

Oopa!

DICK

Mocha!

CHAD

Makin'!

DICK

Kringle!

CHAD

Cripples!

DICK

Shoob!

CHAD

Shoot!

DICK

That's right.

(Chad continues on alone with Dick's encouragement, dancing about with his feet stomping out the rhythm. Dick sits on the bench and flirts with Sam, putting his arm on the bench behind her.)

CHAD

Oopa, makin', cripples, shoot.

DICK

That's good!

CHAD

(He continues. He picks up speed as he gets the hang of it.)
Oopa, makin', cripples, shoot. Oopa, makin' cripples shoot. Oopa, makin' cripples shoot. Is that what you want? Oopa, makin' cripples shoot.

DICK

Good! Now take off all your clothes and proceed to complete 300 pushups!

CHAD

(Chad reaches for the top button of his shirt, then catches himself.)
What? No!

DICK

(Stricken by fear.)
You must! Or the gods will smite us both!

SAM

Just do it, Chad!

CHAD

Wha—? No! This is stupid! I can't take my clothes off in public. I'll get arrested!

DICK

But the gods—

CHAD

I don't even believe in your freakin' gods!!!

DICK

(Stunned silence; Dick sniffs and then sobs like a baby.)
…sniff, sniff … WHHHAAAAAAA!!!!!

SAM

(Dick snuggles up to Sam for comfort. She puts her arms around him.)
Chad, shame on you! Look what you did!

CHAD

What!?

SAM

(To Dick.)
Hey, shhhhh… Aw, it'll be okay. Shhh, calm down, he didn't mean to hurt you.
(He slows his tantrum.)

Do you like coffee?
(Dick stops crying, but continues to whimper and suck his thumb. He then buries his head in Sam's chest for comfort. He nods, acknowledging Sam's comment.)
Well, you just come with me... we'll leave Chad *alone* to deal with the gods by himself.
(Once again coddling Dick.)
It's alright... I know how he can hurt someone's feelings.
(She glares at Chad and exits with Dick clinging to her. Behind Sam's back, Dick flashes a triumphant smirk at Chad.)

CHAD

What? Wait, Sam! Wait a—
(They are gone.)
Damn!
(He sits in despair and confusion over what has just transpired.)

DICK

(Re-enters with the arrowhead in his hands. He gives it to Chad.)
Here, dude, this gets 'em every time!
(He pats Chad on the chest and exits.)

BLACKOUT

True Love

*by Donovan Craft
and Wendy Shockley*

True Love

by Donovan Craft and Wendy Shockley

THE CHARACTERS

John—A young college student.
Sarah—John's rather refined girlfriend.

THE SCENE

The Setting: The living room of a student apartment near a small college campus somewhere south of the Mason-Dixie Line.
The Time: The present.

(At lights up, we see JOHN and SARAH sitting together on John's sofa. They snuggle as they watch a movie on television. John picks up the remote control and mutes the sound.)

JOHN

Sarah?

SARAH

Yes, John? What is it?

JOHN

I was wondering…

SARAH

What?

JOHN

When's the last time you farted?

SARAH

What?!

JOHN

When's the last time you… ya' know… farted?

SARAH

That's disgusting! I'm not talking about that.

JOHN

Why not?

SARAH

…because it's gross. I don't want to sit around and talk about flatulation all night.

JOHN

It's a perfectly natural process.

SARAH

I don't care. My menstrual cycle is a perfectly natural process, too… but you don't wanna talk about that, now do ya?

JOHN

Okay, you're right… but, well then, when's the last time your roommate Tiffany farted?

SARAH

(Deep, frustrating breath.)
I don't know. We don't keep score like you guys do.

JOHN

Come on! Me… and probably the rest of the men on earth… are wondering… because it just seems like… the more I thought about it… the more I realized that I had never been around a woman when she farted… So?

SARAH

So, what?

JOHN

So, when's the last time you or Tiffany had a "rectal eruption?"

SARAH

(Sarcastically and over-exaggerated.)
Oh, I'm not sure… but… Oh! I have an idea! Let's plant a tape recorder in her room so we can document it when she does!

JOHN

Yeah, yeah, yeah!! Then we can get a mathematical count and actually come up with numbers. We could plant tape recorders all over campus and start coming up with averages and sell our info to men all around the world!

SARAH

(Looking excited and shaking her head "yes," then suddenly and very sarcastically changes to negative.)
Ah… no.

JOHN

Come on, all of us guys are starting to think that girls don't break wind.

SARAH

We prefer the term "poot."

JOHN

Well, when was the last time? … If you can't talk about this with your man, then who *can* you talk about it with, huh?

SARAH

You make it sound like… deep down from the inside depths of my colon, I want to divulge some secret information. Well, I don't!

JOHN

What? Do you not love me enough to talk about this?

SARAH

What does love have to do with passing gas?! Of course, I love you!

JOHN

Right, of course… just not enough to talk about this! This is a very important subject that is as near and dear to my heart as you are.

SARAH

Oh, well don't I feel important?! If I tell you, will you be quiet about it so we can just have a pleasant evening?

JOHN

Hmmm, maybe.

SARAH

(To herself.)
I can't believe we are even discussing this.

JOHN

Come on, come on, come on, and tell me already.

SARAH

I don't know… maybe a couple of weeks ago.

JOHN

A couple weeks ago! Wow! I can't imagine! Us guys can barely go a few hours… let alone days or weeks even… How in the world do you hold it in like that?

SARAH

I don't know, we just do! … It's not like we try and keep it in. I guess we just don't create a whole lot of gas to begin with.

JOHN

Geez, that's incredible! Man, I bet when it finally does come out, it's got to be terrible. I'm talking, burn the hairs out of your nose.

SARAH

Stop it.

JOHN

I mean, you'd double your electric bill by hooking up all the fans it would take to just air this place out again... not to mention a million dollars of air freshener—

SARAH

Why don't you just broadcast it to the entire campus? "Attention, pyroclastic flow alert! Please revert to your flower-scented bunkers immediately." I mean... really... Tiffany is just in the other room.

JOHN

I don't care if she hears me! I mean, I'm talking serious major mondo gas. Like, if you tried to light a match, you'd burn your whole dang house down. It would be worse than smelling rottin' eggs with old cabbage, used cooking grease, and my gym socks all rolled into one big bundle with a...
      (She interrupts him.)

SARAH

Shut up, already, you're gonna make me sick!

JOHN

Yeah, and it would be worse than the smell of your vomit, too.
      (She begins hitting him on the head with a box of tissues.)

SARAH

If you don't stop talking about the dang smell... Just be quiet and let's try and enjoy the movie.

JOHN

Okay, okay, calm down. I didn't mean to get you so upset. I'm sorry, Baby. You're right, let's just watch the movie.
      (John leans in and gives her a kiss. With the remote, he ups the volume again and they focus on the movie for a little bit while continuing to snuggle. John looks around

the room deep in thought; Sarah doesn't notice. After a moment of contemplation, John lets out a fart. Sarah reaches for the box of tissues and pulls one out.)

SARAH

God bless you, Baby! Here you go.
    (She hands him the tissue. He mutes the volume again.)

JOHN

Sarah, I didn't sneeze… I let out the great big flowery woof-woof.

SARAH

Oh, my god, you actually tooted in front of me…
    (Sarah moves away from him by sliding to the end of the sofa.)
…next to me, in fact. I thought I felt the couch vibrate.
    (She begins whacking him again with the tissue box.)

JOHN

Baby, listen, I sounded the "trouser trumpets" because I love you.

SARAH

What the hell kinda sense does that make!

JOHN

Stop hitting me and I'll explain.
    (She stops, reluctantly.)
Listen, I "peeled the paint off the wall" to show you that I love you… it shows how comfortable I am around you and that I'm willing to share anything and everything with you.

SARAH

Some things are most definitely not meant to be shared.

JOHN

But listen, Baby, if we can't be open with each other, then how are we ever truly gonna know if we love each other, and if we will be able to live with each other?

SARAH

I don't know… maybe you're right.

JOHN

So, come on, Baby; what do you say?

SARAH

What do I say to what?

JOHN

(With desperation.)
Can you squeeze one out for me to show me how much you love me?

SARAH

You're kidding, right?

JOHN

No, seriously, Baby, come on! Please, show how much you really love me.

SARAH

(She takes a deep breath.)
Fine! …but then we never, ever, ever, ever, ever, revisit this conversation again.

JOHN

(Very excited.)
Sure, fine, absolutely; what ever you want, Baby!
(Sarah has a look of absolute strain on her face while trying to let one go. Then all of a sudden she stops straining and smiles confidently.)

SARAH

There you go; now, can we drop it?

JOHN

What are you talking about? I never heard anything. Baby, I want to hear or feel something. I wanted you to "drop the bomb," "give the toothless speech," "cut the cheese…" I mean, I wanted a "real cheek flapper." Come on, "let loose the iron giant!" Something!

SARAH

John?

JOHN

Yeah?

SARAH

You forgot one.

JOHN

I did?

SARAH

S. B. D. "Silent but deadly."
  (John takes a sniff and reacts, almost fainting.)

JOHN

Oh, Baby! You do love me!
  (They move in together and hug.)

BLACKOUT

Miss Tranquility

by Pamela Darnell and Meg Elliot

Miss Tranquility
by Pamela Darnell and Meg Elliot

THE CHARACTERS

Melissa—A petite, female yoga instructor, twenty something. She has a calm and soothing voice with refined physical mannerisms.
Tiger—A big, buff, arrogant male in his twenties.
Kitty and Josie—Two attractive females, twenty-something, participating in Melissa's yoga class.

THE SCENE

The Setting: The exercise area of a suburban health club.
The Time: The present.

(At lights up, we see MELISSA and her two students KITTY and JOSIE in the middle of yoga class, seated on mats in a stretching position. Along with other workout items, a punching bag is standing prominently on the other end of the stage.)

MELISSA

(Soothing.)
Alright, beautiful job, ladies. Now, raise your arms slowly… slowly above your head. Hold it there… breathe in… now, exhale. Doesn't this feel great? Oh, I need this today.
(TIGER enters and begins using punching bag loudly. He listens to music through sports head phones.)
Whenever you are ready, stand to your feet and we will begin the Warrior II sequence, or Virabhadrasana.
(Tiger begins grunting with each punch.)
Let's take a large step out to the side, point your left foot towards the front of the room, and extend your arms out. Good…
(Tiger continues to punch and grunt while Melissa and the girls attempt to ignore him.)
Now, gently, oh so gently, le-e-e-ean over until you can't stretch any more, then slowly tip at the waist and place your left hand down by your calf, or ankle, or wherever is comfortable for you. This is called Trikonasana.
(Tiger begins humming his own theme music, something like the Rocky theme. Melissa calmly excuses herself and walks over to Tiger.)

Excuse me, sir. If you don't mind, we are trying to have class over here.

TIGER

(He removes his headphones.)
Huh?

MELISSA

I'm trying to teach a class.

TIGER

Yeah, so?

MELISSA

You're being a little too loud.

TIGER

Hey, lady, it's a free country.
(Melissa throws him a look of disgust and returns to the yoga pose.)

MELISSA

Now, at your next inhale, bend your left knee so that it's at a ninety degree angle directly above your foot… and straighten up at the waist… into Virabhadrasana. Now breathe… enjoy the moment…
(Tiger is still punching and grunting, Melissa grows more annoyed.)
Focus on your inner soul… that peaceful and quiet place… think calm and tranquil thoughts—
(Tiger begins talking trash to the punching bag.)

TIGER

Yeah, you like that?! Ungh! Want some more of that?! You ain't got nothin'!

MELISSA

Peace… tranquility…

TIGER

Heck yeah; that's right! Momma said, knock you out!

(Melissa is frustrated and walks back over to Tiger.)

MELISSA

Excuse me. Sir, you are still disturbing my class. Please try to keep it down.

TIGER

Lady, do you know who I am? I mean, do you have any idea who you're talking to?

MELISSA

No, and I don't particularly care. You're being very disrespectful.

TIGER

You really don't recognize me?

MELISSA

No. I really don't.

TIGER

Seriously.

MELISSA

I am dead serious.

TIGER

I'm Tiger! Kickboxer extraordinaire.
  (Melissa gives him a blank stare.)
I was in every single one of the Tae Bo videos. Back row, in the far left corner. Billy Blanks is my close personal friend.

MELISSA

Well, that's great. But I don't care *who* you are. You're ruining my yoga class.

TIGER

Geez, who peed in your corn flakes this morning?

(Melissa returns to the girls, but is still annoyed.)

MELISSA

Okay. Great job, class. Can you feel it?
(The girls nod.)
Wonderful. Now it's time to enter into our meditation phase. Let's have a seat in the Lotus position.
(Tiger begins to get loud again.)
Good… okay, now rest your hands on your knees, connect the thumb and middle finger in a circle…

TIGER

(Speaking again to the punching bag.)
Ungh! That's what I thought, you piece of crap!

MELISSA

Now, close your eyes, and try to shut out everything around you… Listen to your inner spirit… Imagine you are sitting on a beautiful sandy beach… waves gently lapping at your toes…

TIGER

Boo-yah!! Who's your Daddy!!

MELISSA

(Angry, she stands up and crosses to him.)
Listen, Bobcat, or whatever your name is, how are we supposed to achieve inner peace with you being so obnoxious over here!?
(The two girls stay seated throughout this argument. They occasionally open their eyes and glance around uncomfortably.)

TIGER

First of all, it's *Tiger*. And second, some of us are trying to have a *real* workout, unlike that pansy yoga crap you're doing.

MELISSA

Pansy yoga crap!? I'll have you know that Ashtanga yoga is a serious discipline that is a lot more challenging than it looks!

TIGER

Pfffff! Whatever. Kickboxing is where it's at.

MELISSA

I bet *you* can't do it.

TIGER

What did you say?

MELISSA

(Mocking.)
Mr. "Kickboxer extraordinaire," I bet you can't do *half* the poses we're doing.

TIGER

Ha! Like I'd be caught dead doing yoga. It's freakin' un-American. It's not even a sport!

MELISSA

Fine, if you're scared…

TIGER

Scared?

MELISSA

You heard me.

TIGER

You're full of crap! I ain't scared!

MELISSA

I think you are.

TIGER

I ain't scared of nothin'!

MELISSA

Then why don't you come prove it?

TIGER

Well maybe I will!

MELISSA

Bring it!

(Tiger gets a mat and joins the two girls. Melissa is still flustered, but calming down.)

Alright class. Now let's work on our balancing poses.

(The girls stand.)

We'll start with the tree.

(The girls do the move with perfect precision; Tiger does it very awkwardly.)

Place the sole of your left foot on your right inner thigh. Good... now palms together in front of your chest in the prayer position... Concentrate your energy... starting down at your right foot... then all the way up to your head and through your fingertips.

(She raises her arms above her head still in prayer position. Tiger keeps flailing and hopping and losing balance, struggling to still look cool for the ladies. He winks at them when they glare in his direction.)

Tiger, is there a problem?

TIGER

Nope! Nothin' to it. I could do this all day.

MELISSA

Good. Keep concentrating on sending your energy upwards, shooting out through your fingertips like tiny sparkling rays of light...

(Melissa begins to lose her balance.)

TIGER

Oh ho! So the calm and tranquil yoga instructor can't even do it!

MELISSA

Sshhh!
(Melissa stumbles again and catches herself quickly.)

TIGER

(Taunting.)
Oh, Big Bad Yoga Chick can't even hold her own! Come on, just picture that sandy beach you were blabbing about.

MELISSA

(Embarrassed.)
Shut up!

TIGER

You can do it, become the lotus blossom… feel the rays of sunshine!

MELISSA

That's it! I've had it! Class is dismissed early today!
(The two girls pick up their mats and exit. Tiger moves back in front of the punching bag as the girls leave. Melissa turns to Tiger in a rage.)
You… you've ruined my yoga class!

TIGER

Well, *you* ruined my workout! Guess that makes us even.

MELISSA

(With growing anger.)
I have never been so angry at another human being *in my life!*

TIGER

Oh yeah? You wanna do something about it?

MELISSA

I know violence is never the answer, but I just want to punch you in the face!

TIGER

Oh, wait. Little Miss Tranquility is probably too good to express her anger, right?

MELISSA

In your case, I will gladly make an exception!
(Melissa reaches back and lets a punch fly towards Tiger. He ducks out of the way and she hits the punching bag. He straightens up.)

TIGER

Oh yeah, just as I thought! … You hit like a girl!

MELISSA

Aaaargh!! Take that!
(Melissa lets another punch fly, and once again, Tiger ducks and Melissa hits the punching bag. Tiger moves out of the way as Melissa continues to take her aggression out on the punching bag. Tiger moves over to Melissa's yoga mat and sits down.)

TIGER

Whew… all this exercise can wear a dude out.
(Tiger crosses his legs. He rests his hands on his knees and closes his eyes. Melissa is still grunting and punching away at the bag.)

MELISSA

Yeah, that's right! I got your inner peace right here! Come and get it!

TIGER

Mmm… yeah… sandy beach…

MELISSA

You want some more?! Yeah! Who's your momma?!

BLACKOUT

Fortress of Solitude

by Rachel Jones
and George Harrison Hendricks IV

Fortress of Solitude

by Rachel Jones
and George Harrison Hendricks IV

THE CHARACTERS

Janney—A recent college graduate; a free spirit.
Scott—A college graduate; a neat-freak with a controlling sort of personality.

THE SCENE

The Setting: Janney's room in the apartment she sub-lets from Scott in Auburn, Alabama.
The Time: The present.

(At lights up, we see JANNEY sitting on the floor in her room reading. Her room is ultimately messy; it looks as if a dump truck has emptied its contents into the middle of her room and wild monkeys have spread it all around. Janney has cleared a space in the middle of the room to sit. Under the pile there is evidence of a bed and a night stand. After a moment, SCOTT enters from the hallway. He carries a box under his arm. He holds his cell phone to his ear.)

JANNEY

Hey, what are you doing with that box?
(Preoccupied with his phone call, he shifts the box so that he can give her a hand signal that he'll be off in a moment.)

SCOTT

Yeah, Pete. I know you're in a hard place. I'll see what I can do. Talk to you later. Bye.
(Scott looks at Janney.)
Sorry, I was on the phone. What's up?

JANNEY

What's with the box?

SCOTT

I'm cleaning. Today's Goodwill day, remember?

JANNEY

How could I forget? Why do you think I'm in here?
(Janney looks at the box incredulously.)
Is that stuff from your room?

SCOTT

(With subtle sarcasm.)
No, I went into your room when you weren't looking and cleaned it out.

JANNEY

(Surprised.)
What?

SCOTT

I'm kidding. Although, I'm half tempted to wait 'til you go to work and take a bulldozer to this place.

JANNEY

Don't joke about such things. You nearly gave me a heart attack.

SCOTT

Even if I were to clean your room, Janney, I wouldn't know where to begin. The President of the United States would take one look at this room and declare it a disaster area.

JANNEY

(Looks confused.)
Why would the President come to see my room?
(She shrugs her shoulders and goes back to reading.)

SCOTT

Never mind. But seriously, you need to clean your room. The landlord would have a fit if he saw it.

JANNEY

There's nothing wrong with my room. Trust me. I know where everything is.

SCOTT

No, I'm pretty sure you don't. I mean, look at this place!
(He picks up a pile of clothes and sees a pizza box. He picks up the box and studies it.)
You don't eat pizza. You *hate* pizza!
(Janney, who has lost all interest in conversation, has begun reading again.)

JANNEY

(She's still looking at the book.)
Huh? Oh… I do hate pizza. Ever since graduation. Remember that? You were there, holding my hair. The puke was coming so fast, it was spewing out of my nose and…

SCOTT

Ugh! Gross! You don't need to remind me. You said I was there. I still have nightmares about that.
(Pauses. Realization.)
Wait a minute. That was six months ago.
(Janney looks up from the book as if caught up in her memories.)

JANNEY

Oh, yeah.
(Janney pauses and shudders.)
I can remember it as if it were yesterday. Ugh!
(Scott drops the box and puts the clothes over the pizza box in disgust.)

SCOTT

Okay, I know we've had talks about this before… and I know you've limited the mess to just your room…
(Janney looks up from her book, beaming with pride.)
But this… this… I just can't take it!
(Janney's smile drops.)

JANNEY

But it's *my* room. My sanctuary. You can't come into it and wreck my fortress of solitude! Who do you think you are? Magneto?

SCOTT

That's Lex Luther... and it looks like you've done a good job of "wrecking" already. Are the piles of laundry supposed to be the walls?

JANNEY

Ah-ha! I'll have you know, I know where everything is. Go ahead, test me, if you'd like.

SCOTT

What?
(Janney gets up off the floor.)

JANNEY

You heard me. Give me an item... any item in my room... and I can give you directions on where to find it. If it's not within a ten-inch radius of the site I directed you to, I'll clean my room to meet even your obsessive-compulsive standards.

SCOTT

I am not obsessive—
(Janney sticks out her hand.)

JANNEY

Take it, or leave, Interloper!
(Scott pauses. He looks at the room and then quickly grabs her hand.)

SCOTT

I'll take it. But, I get to choose the items.

JANNEY

That's not fair. You don't know what's in here.

SCOTT

Yes, I do.

JANNEY

Do not.

SCOTT

Do, too.

JANNEY

Says who?

SCOTT

Says my obsessive-compulsive behavior. How about this? If I choose something that is not in here, you get to choose the items from there on out.

JANNEY

Fine.
(Scott rubs his hands together and looks around.)

SCOTT

Alright. Let's start with my CDs you borrowed last month.

JANNEY

Oh, please, that's easy. Over to the left, on top of my nightstand. They're under my science project.
(Scott crosses to the nightstand. He picks up the glass between finger and thumb, holding it a good distance away from him. The glass has grass and dirt crusted onto it.)

SCOTT

What is this?

JANNEY

My science project...

(Janney crosses to Scott and takes the glass from him. She holds it up to the light.) It's almost finished.

SCOTT

You graduated college six months ago, Janney.
(Janney looks at him matter-of-factly.)

JANNEY

You should never give up learning, Scott. Besides, you're missing the point. Your CDs are right there.
(Scott picks up the CD cases.)

SCOTT

Ha! Finally, I get these back. Now, where are your dirty clothes?
(Janney opens her mouth to tell him.)
No, wait. Lemme guess. All over the place, right?
(Janney carefully puts the glass back on the nightstand. She folds her arms and walks back over to her book.)

JANNEY

Nope. Under the bed.

SCOTT

What?

JANNEY

Under my bed.

SCOTT

Why would you put your dirty clothes under your bed?

JANNEY

I can't stand the sight of dirty things.
(Scott looks around the room in disbelief.)

SCOTT

And yet you can stand *this?!*

JANNEY

Stand what?

SCOTT

This… this… mess…

JANNEY

It's not a mess. It's organized in a highly specific geometric configuration called "a pile," my dear roomie. Besides, organization is for people too lazy to look for things.
(Scott throws up his hands in disbelief. He turns to leave and stubs his toe on something hard.)

SCOTT

Augh!!
(Janney drops the book and walks quickly over to him. She puts her hands on his shoulders and rubs them.)

JANNEY

Now, now… easy does it. You know, you should relax. Stress shortens your lifespan.
(Scott shakes Janney's hands off him.)

SCOTT

I'm not stressed! I stubbed my toe…
(Scott bends down and picks up a conch shell.)
…on this!
(Janney claps her hands together and laughs.)

JANNEY

Oh, there you are!

SCOTT

I can *not* take this anymore! You're cleaning this stuff out! Our agreement is going out the window along with this safety hazard!
 (Janney grabs the conch shell away from Scott.)

JANNEY

No! She's my friend!

SCOTT

Excuse me?

JANNEY

You've heard of pet rocks, right? Well, she's my pet conch.

SCOTT

That's the stupidest thing I've ever heard
 (Janney gasps and covers the conch shell.)

JANNEY

Shhhh! You're hurting Conchie's feelings. She's got ears, you know.

SCOTT

Where?
 (Pause.)
How do you know it's a girl?
 (Thinks about it.)
Regardless of the sex, it's *not* a real pet.

JANNEY

Conchie is, too!

SCOTT

Oh, and what's her talent? Imitating the ocean?

JANNEY

(In awe.)
How did you know?
(Scott sighs.)

SCOTT

That thing is an accident waiting to happen. Look what it did to my toe!

JANNEY

She didn't mean to. We were playing hide-and-seek before you came in here…
and you found her. Congrats! Now, it's your turn to hide.
(Janney shoves Scott towards the door.)
Go on now… go! We'll count to thirty-five.
(Scott is halfway out the door before he realizes what he's doing.)

SCOTT

Janney!!
(Janney, who has started back towards her book, cringes and slowly turns to face him.)

JANNEY

You're yelling at me. You…
(She looks as though she's about to cry.)
…you've never yelled at me before.
(Scott sighs.)

SCOTT

Janney…
(Janney "breaks down" into tears. Scott sighs and crosses to her. He puts his arms around her.)
I… I'm sorry. It's just that you… you really need to clean this place up. It's not healthy to have such a messy room.
(Janney looks up at him and wipes her face.)

JANNEY

If… if you really want me to, I will, but… but…

(Scott loosens his embrace and looks down at her.)

SCOTT

But, what?

JANNEY

It's my fortress. My own... my... my fortress of solitude.

SCOTT

Oh, for crying out...
  (Janney shoves him.)

JANNEY

Besides, you're slowly trying to change me! You... you... I see what you're doing! You're... you're *The Man!* Oh... first it was "just" the living room, then the bathroom, now it's my room... What's next? ... Am I next?
  (Accusingly.)
You're an agent of "The Establishment" trying to keep me down! Are you going to attempt to change me into some stuffy Hollister and Fitch girl? So that's why you bought me that hideous shirt for Christmas!

SCOTT

That's *Abercrombie* and Fitch...

JANNEY

Stuff it, Whitey!! You want to change me! Now I'm prisoner in my own fortress! How dare you!

SCOTT

Oh, for crying out loud! I'm not trying to change you! I just wanted you to tidy up a bit.

JANNEY

Whatever you say, Warden. You can take away my space, my fortress, but you can't take... *my freedom!!*

SCOTT

Whoa, William Wallace! Chill!

JANNEY

You know what? I'm sick of this! Conchie and I... we're leaving. I won't take anymore of this... this heterozigation!

SCOTT

Don't you mean, homogenization?

JANNEY

WHATEVER!!!!
(Janney begins to storm out of her room.)

SCOTT

Janney, wait. Please don't go. I didn't realize you hated that gift. You can take it back for a refund. You're a great apartment-mate. I can get past this messy room thing, honest.

JANNEY

No, it's over pal. You're taking over *my* fortress. I put up with the overtaking of the living room and even kept the bathroom clean. This was the last straw! This bird is flying the coop!

SCOTT

Please, Janney, please!
(Scott gets on his knees.)
I'm begging you. The lease is up tomorrow! I can't afford this place by myself. I've no place to go!

JANNEY

Well, you should've thought about that before you laid siege!
(Janney grabs her conch.)
Come on, Conchie, we'll get our stuff when the *Warden* leaves his post.

(Janney gives Scott the evil eye and then exits. Scott bows his head and covers his face in defeat. He waits until he hears the door slam. He then looks up and gets his cell phone out and dials a number.)

SCOTT

Hello, Pete?

(Beat.)

Yeah, like a charm. I've already got your first box in here. She'll move her stuff out tomorrow while I'm at work.

(Beat.)

Hey, yeah, I know I'm good. Glad to help you out. Yep, see you tomorrow, man. Later.

(Scott hangs up the cell phone. Lights fade to black.)

BLACKOUT

In the Beginning

by George Harrison Hendricks IV

In The Beginning

by George Harrison Hendricks IV

THE CHARACTERS

The Director—A megalomaniac with anger issues.
Byron—A theater technician responsible for the light board.
The Bicycle Girl (Felicia)—A teenage girl.

THE SCENE

The Setting: The stage of the theater belonging to the Ronkonkoma Township Theatrical Society.
The Time: The present… perhaps.

(Stage is dark except for a single spotlight casting a field of stars across the stage floor. The theme from 2001: A Space Odyssey *plays before THE DIRECTOR interrupts from a seat in the audience.)*

THE DIRECTOR

Okay, okay, okay, kill the music! This isn't working. Why isn't it working? Someone bring up the lights. Lights? *Lights!*
(Light shines center stage, awaiting someone to fill the void.)
Thank you, Byron.

BYRON

(From the light board, offstage.)
S'alright
(The Director enters from audience center; he climbs on the stage and moves into the light.)

THE DIRECTOR

Can someone please tell me what I was thinking? Honestly folks, can someone give me a clue?
(Looks off left and right.)
Anyone? Anyone?! *Anyone?!* I am at a complete loss here, people. Who in their right mind would not only come up with the idea to reenact the creation of the universe on stage, but think it was a *good* idea? I can't blame drugs. I haven't

touched anything stronger than baby aspirin since waking up in that Mexican cemetery back in the late eighties. It was a harrowing experience, and I'm almost positive that Gary Coleman was lying when he told me that... Byron! Give me more light, please.

(There is a small shift in light intensity.)

More.

(Again a small rise in intensity.)

Mooooore.

(And again.)

All the way, Byron! I want lights up, not sunrise!

(Lights blaze, causing the Director to wince.)

Thank you, Byron.

BYRON

S'alright

(From now on, whenever the lights are brought up, they slowly start to dim.)

THE DIRECTOR

Where was I? Oh... yes. Well, my mother said to always leave an audience wanting more. Ahhhh... My mother. Mommy warned me not to take on more than I could handle. "Don't worry," I said. "It's only creation. Reaching beyond your grasp is the stepping stone to greatness," I said. I should have listened. Ohhhhh, I should have *listened!* She was right about the Flo-Bee; she was right about Crystal Pepsi...; she even predicted David Hasselhoff's singing career before it reached critical mass! But this wasn't the "easy-come, easy-go" consumer fad-market... this wasn't the fickle world of German demagoguery... this was a stage production! You can't quantify the magic that happens when a group of people get together and decide to create something out of nothing. There isn't a way to predict that which has no basis in reality until it becomes reality. That's the beauty of it. The downside is... in this case, at least... once it becomes a reality, you're pretty much screwed.

(Felicia rides by left to right on a bicycle; she rings her bike bell twice.)

I thought I told you to leave that thing outside!

(Her bell answers him again rudely.)

Jiminy Christmas.... I *had* to hire Union.

(Yells after Felicia.)

What do you *do*, anyway?

(No answer.)

You see what I have to work with around here? Twenty-six people on the tech crew and I couldn't tell you a single one of their names. *Twenty-six!* There were only half that many disciples and look what they got accomplished! I could probably tell you *their* names.

(Begins to name Disciples on his fingers.)

Lessee... Judas, Peter, Matthew, Mark, John, Paul... George... Ringo wasn't one, was he?

(Gets no answer; scowls and huffs.)

Never mind! They're all dead and I'm not, so let's not dwell. As I was saying, it's amazing the kind of things one can get accomplished when they *have decent help!!*

(Looks left and right; and again. He notices that the lights have dimmed considerably.)

Speaking of... Either my diabetes has finally caught up to my eyes... or my illustrious lighting tech has just burst a major vessel in his brain and is lying upon the light board causing the light to flee my stage as the light of life is fleeing from his body! Byron! Byron! Byron!! Are you dead?! Should I go out and buy a Seeing Eye Dog or should I don a black armband in memory of you?! Buddy, if you don't get those lights back up posthaste, we will all be doing the armband *regardless of my eyesight!*

(Lights blaze to full again.)

Thank you, Byron!!

BYRON

S'alright

(There is snickering heard from backstage. The Director glares.)

THE DIRECTOR

Silence! I said, SILENCE! That's it. You are all on your own. You... PEOPLE... can just *rot* for all I care! You and your, your, your... stupid... *Ass-faces!*

(Begins patting himself down in search of his keys.)

I'm out of here! Where the deuce are my keys?!

(Pauses mid-pat. Thinks. Remembers.)

Oh, yes.... I don't have a car.

(Mutters.)

How was I supposed to know that 'Open Container' included beer helmets?

(Gets an idea.)

Oh... umm... *What's her name... what's her name... what's her name...* Ohhh. ummm, Bicycle Girl! May I borrow your... umm... conveyance? Your transportation. Your wheels. What? I refuse to call it that. No. *No!* I said... *Fine!* May I please borrow your "Phat Ride"? What do you mean, no?! Rent it? Why, I never... Forget it. I won't sully myself with your tainted mode of transport! The Bard walked, Jesus walked, and *so... shall... I!*

(Pace dimming of the light to match speed of the monologue.)

Friends, Critics, Paying Customers, I fear I must bid you all adieu. It seems my genius is not needed here. I know you all paid good money to come and see the brilliance of my mind unfold before you in prose and set, but I see it cannot come to pass. The starving dogs nipping at my heels have decided to envy my genius instead of bringing it to suckle at the bosom of their creative collective. They feel that it is better to destroy my vision in the womb rather than rear it as their own and see that it gets into the finest schools and meets a nice girl to have its own brood of preternaturally brilliant baby visions.

(Takes a moment to coo and make silly faces at the imaginary "grandchildren.")

Anyway, I digress. The long and short of it is this: I cannot work in an environment that bears such ill will towards me and the fruit which I long to bear for you fine people. I am through with the teeming pit of vipers that is the Ronkonkoma Township Theatrical Society. Furthermore, I would like to...

(Lights reach a noticeable level of dim.)

BYYYRRROOOOONNNNN!!!!! Oh, honestly now.

(Lights fade completely to black. He speaks from the darkness.)

I fail to find the humor in this! Byron! Byron? Hello? ... Anyone?

(Crickets chirp. Silence. Music starts up. 2001: A Space Odyssey *builds. Star field lights come up once again. Stage center, where the Director was last seen, stands a large black monolith lit by an impressive down light. Music swells to conclusion.)*

BLACKOUT

It's the Thought that Counts

by Jeremy Kerr
with Noelle DeLozier

It's the Thought that Counts

by Jeremy Kerr
with Noelle DeLozier

THE CHARACTERS

Heath—A handsome young man in his early twenties; a college student.
Kim—Heath's girlfriend of many years; she is an attractive young woman in her early twenties.

THE SCENE

The Setting: The living room of Heath's suburban apartment.
The Time: The present.

(At lights up, we see KIM sitting on a sofa in a very average looking living room; there is a coffee table, an end table, and an occasional chair. Kim is reading. Enter HEATH through the main door. He is returning from a shopping trip and carries a large shopping bag; a box is visible at the top of the bag.)

HEATH

Hi, Kim! Happy birthday!

KIM

Awww… Heath, Baby, you remembered.

HEATH

Of course, I remembered! You wrote it on my calendar.

KIM

Weeeell…

HEATH

…and you programmed it into my phone.

KIM

So it worked? The alarm went off?

HEATH

In the middle of class. Dr. Bottoms threw a dry-erase marker at me.

KIM

Well, I didn't want you to forget.

HEATH

Anyway, I wouldn't have forgotten. I love you too much.
   (They kiss.)
But you can't have your present until after we go out to eat.

KIM

Out to eat?

HEATH

Yep. I'm taking you out for a birthday dinner.

KIM

You're so sweet.
   (She gives him a hug.)

HEATH

Let me go change shirts and I'll be right back.
   (He exits. She begins eyeing the bag. She crosses to it, careful to make sure that Heath isn't returning. She peeks into the sack, hoping to get a look at her birthday present. She speaks loudly in an effort to mask the sound of rustling paper.)

KIM

So where are you taking me?

HEATH

   (Offstage.)
Taco Bell!

KIM

(Distracted. Taking the box out of the bag.)
Uh-huh. That sounds good.

HEATH

(Offstage.)
No! I'm kidding. I'm taking you to this new place in town. You like Italian food, don't you?

KIM

(Having opened the box, she pulls out the most hideous dress imaginable. She speaks loudly to herself, paying Heath's question no mind.)
No!

HEATH

(Off.)
What? I thought you did.

KIM

I mean, yeah. I like Italian… I just…
(To herself, holding dress up.)
Ugh!

HEATH

(Coming onstage.)
Does this shirt look okay?

KIM

(She shoves the dress back into the box and the box back into the bag. She pretends that nothing is wrong.)
Uh-huh. Fine.

HEATH

Good. So what did you see today?

KIM

(Thinking she has been caught.)
Nothing! I didn't see anything!

HEATH

Really? I thought you were going to the museum with your art class.

KIM

Oh… yeah. We did. We, uh… Heath, we need to talk.

HEATH

Uh-oh. Those four words are the kiss of death to a relationship.

KIM

No, I just want to talk about… about how well we know each other.

HEATH

We know each other. I think that when we get back and you see your present you'll agree… I know what you like.

KIM

Riiiiiight. About that birthday present—

HEATH

Kim, you'll be so proud of me. I mean, I don't want to give the surprise away, but I spent a long time searching for it. It wasn't just some spur of the moment purchase.

KIM

It wasn't?

HEATH

Oh, no! I put a lot of thought into this. I looked online, I looked in catalogues, I checked all the stores to see what was in style—okay, I'm about to say too much. I don't want you to guess. Let's just say I think you'll like it and I hope it fits.

KIM

(Beat.)
Yeah, we need to talk. I've decided you shouldn't get me anything for my birthday.

HEATH

But I already did.

KIM

Well, you should take it back.

HEATH

But—

KIM

Take it back!

HEATH

Kim, this is important... if for no other reason than it's your birthday. You get presents on your birthday, whether you like it or not.

KIM

Well, dinner can be my present.

HEATH

What? No, dinner's dinner. This is a big deal to me. I went and picked this out on my own. For the last four years I've asked your mom or your sister what I should get you, but this time it was me. All on my own. And I spent good money on this, too.

KIM

Not too much, I hope.

HEATH

How much isn't the point. The point is... I love you and I wanted to get you something you'll like.

KIM

But I don't!

HEATH

What?

KIM

I said, "What if I don't?"

HEATH

Oh, you will. Like I said earlier... I know you. I know what you like and don't like.

KIM

Oh, really?

HEATH

Yeah. Now come on, let's go eat.

KIM

Fine. Okay.
    (They exit. After about three seconds, Kim re-enters.)
I can't!

HEATH

(Re-entering.)
Kim! What are you doing?

KIM

Look, I've been thinking a lot lately about where we're headed with this relationship.

HEATH

Good! Me, too.

KIM

I mean, five years—you know?

HEATH

I know. That's what I'm saying.

KIM

And today... well, all week, to be truthful... I just... I don't think this is gonna work. I don't think you even know me.

HEATH

What? Sure I do.

KIM

Heath, I already know what the gift is.

HEATH

You do?

KIM

Yes.
   (Beat.)
And I don't want it.

HEATH

What? Are you... are you serious?

KIM

It's ugly.

HEATH

It's gorgeous!

KIM

Oh, my gosh, Heath, it's hideous. I can't believe you spent a long time looking for it. I can't believe you spent five seconds looking for it. What...? Did somebody throw it out?

HEATH

(Very hurt.)
I... Look, if... I mean, even if you think it's not the prettiest in the world, surely what it stands for means—

KIM

What it stands for? It stands for how little you truly know me.

HEATH

How can you say that?

KIM

Okay, the fact that you wanted to shop without asking my mom or sister is nice. That means something to me... But what you came up with...? It's ridiculous.

HEATH

I just thought that's where we were headed.

KIM

Headed where? Goodwill?

HEATH

Goodwill?! No, marriage!

KIM

Marriage? I hope you do not think I'm getting married in that. Who are you? I don't know you. And you *obviously* don't know me!

HEATH

Okay, maybe I'm just being a guy, but I thought this is what girls wanted...
What I'm *supposed* to do!

KIM

What girls wanted? You think I wanted this?
    (She yanks the dress out of the box.)

HEATH

No, this.
    (He holds up a ring box.)
I was going to ask you to marry me after dinner.

KIM

    (Long pause as she realizes what he has said. She holds up the dress.)
Well, what's this?

HEATH

The present from your mom. She isn't going to be able to come over tonight.

KIM

Oh. Well.
    (Drops the dress back into the bag.)
Very well.

HEATH

So what do I do with this ring?

KIM

    (As she speaks, she draws close to him.)
Well... if you don't mind being married to a crazy woman who tends to over-
react, I'll take it.

HEATH

On one condition.

KIM

What's that?

HEATH

Promise you'll never wear that dress.
(They kiss. Lights fade.)

BLACKOUT

Social Distortion

by Micheal S. Pardue
with Stephanie Faile

Social Distortion

by Micheal S. Pardue
with Stephanie Faile

THE CHARACTERS

Sam—He is a reputable young man; early twenties. He is very innocent, although he often finds himself in circumstances to the contrary.
Jenn—Sam's girlfriend; early twenties. She is beyond any modern sense of innocence. She loves Sam deeply and trusts him, even if she catches him in acts that seemingly would break that trust.

THE SCENE

The Setting: A park.
The Time: The present.

(At lights up, we see an empty park bench. SAM and JENN enter; Sam is carrying two empty pizza boxes.)

JENN

Thanks for bringing me to the park, Sweetie.

SAM

You're welcome.

JENN

What are those boxes for?

SAM

Well, I couldn't find my mom's big blanket, so I brought these so we wouldn't have to sit on a wet bench.

JENN

Great.
(Sam lays the packages on the park bench and Jenn sits; Sam remains standing.)

SAM

Listen; there is something I've been wanting to talk to you about.

JENN

(Smiling.)
Okay.

SAM

We've been seeing each other for a long time now… years even.

JENN

It's been three years, four months, five days and eleven minutes…
(Looks at her watch.)
…make that twelve.

SAM

And it's been a lot of fun, right?

JENN

Sure 'nuff.

SAM

As a matter of fact, it was right here that we met.

JENN

Oh, my gosh! You're right, it was. You had O.D.ed on over-the-counter painkill-ers and passed out on this very bench.

SAM

I had thought it was odd that the package said to take six at a time.

JENN

Six at a time; six times a day—same thing. You did look awful nasty on that bench, though.

SAM

True... but wasn't it romantic? The moon, the stars, the...

JENN

...vomit.

(Slightly uneasy. Pause.)

SAM

We connected on a level that I had never experienced with another person before. I was just blown away by how smart and great and... well... just how wonderful you are.

JENN

I know... I still can't believe I helped you that night. I thought you were one of those nasty homeless guys, but when I looked into your glazed-over eyes, I knew that you were the one for me.

SAM

And I didn't turn out to be too much of a nasty pill-popper, now did I?

JENN

Nope.

SAM

From then until now we've been right beside each other... like the time we went skiing in Colorado with your friends.

JENN

Oh, I had such a good time... although I would have gotten to spend more time with you, if we hadn't played hide-and-seek with Angie. I looked for you two for hours... If I had only found you sooner, you two wouldn't have had to cuddle up behind that tree to stay warm.

SAM

It's survival-of-the-fittest out in the cold.

JENN

That was the same ski trip you went down the mountain into town with Emily for supplies. It was so crazy, ya'll getting stuck.

SAM

That night was so strange.

JENN

You guys had to get hotel rooms because the snow was so bad you couldn't come back to the cabin.

SAM

I have just never seen it snow so much, so quickly. We just couldn't run the risk of trying to drive back.

JENN

It was so odd; it didn't even snow up at the cabin.

SAM

Nature can be a weird thing sometimes.

JENN

True…

SAM

I did manage a little luck, though.

JENN

(Thinking for a moment.)
Oh, yeah, that's right; the hotel only charged you for one room. I was kinda upset at first… I mean… you two… one room… so many bad thoughts… but you explained it must have been a computer error. I knew deep down nothing was

going on, although Angie seemed strangely upset the entire time ya'll were gone. She must have just been worried; she does that sometimes.

SAM

I really got to know your friends on that trip.

JENN

That is one of the reasons we are so compatible. You always seem to warm right up to all my friends: Amy, Lauren, Bridget, Alison, Annie, Rachel, Beth... the list could go on and on. They all talk about you constantly. They always want to see you and talk with you on the phone when they are at my house.

SAM

I enjoy being with your friends. They're great girls.

JENN

And you are a great guy.

SAM

Most of the time.
(They giggle.)

JENN

You warmed up to Joanna, too. My sister has never gotten along with any of my boyfriends until she met you.

SAM

I try.

JENN

She is practically in love with you... in a totally platonic way, of course.

SAM

...of course.

JENN

She always wants to go to the park with you and invite you over, even when I am not at home. It means so much to me that you spend so much time with her.

SAM

Oh, she's a sweet girl, I don't mind at all. It really works out in both our favors.
   (Pause.)

JENN

So, what did you want to talk about?

SAM

   (Day dreaming.)
What?

JENN

You said you wanted to talk about something.

SAM

Oh, yeah, well, I have been doing a lot of thinking recently… you know, about us…

JENN

Yes?

SAM

…how we connect…

JENN

Go on…

SAM

…how we get along…

JENN

And?

SAM

(Mustering up enough courage.)
...I think we should take the next step.

JENN

(Excited.)
Really?

SAM

Yes, we're in love, Honey, and when two people have shared as much as we have, they have to take the next big step.

JENN

I totally agree.

SAM

I am so glad you're with me on this.

JENN

I have been waiting for this for years!

SAM

Me, too!
(He starts to move close to her.)

JENN

You have to ask first.

SAM

Will you...

JENN

Go on!

SAM

Will you…

JENN

You can do it.

SAM

Will you let me kiss you?!

JENN

Yes! Yes, you may!
(They awkwardly share an embrace and a quick peck on the lips. For a moment, they sit in silence, both slightly embarrassed and excited. Sam looks at his watch.)

SAM

Don't you have to go to work?

JENN

Oh, you're right!
(She stands up.)
What are you going to do now?

SAM

I'm having dinner with your mother.

JENN

(Clueless.)
Okay, have fun, Sweetie Pie.

SAM

Don't worry, I will. You're the best.

(Jenn exits left. Sam sits back down on the bench with a smile of innocent contentment on his face.)

BLACKOUT

Study Time

*by Amber M. Jackson
and Michael Mitteer*

Study Time

by Amber M. Jackson
and Michael Mitteer

THE CHARACTERS

Kelly—An attractive, female college student. Very sweet.
Cal—An average male college student. Very handsome.

THE SCENE

The Setting: A university dorm lobby with sofas and chairs and study tables.
The Time: The present.

(Lights up. We see a dorm lobby; the chairs and sofas are mostly empty. CAL studies on the sofa. After a moment, KELLY enters. She spies Cal and decides to approach him.)

KELLY

Hi, what are you doing?

CAL

Studying.

KELLY

Me, too. Doesn't it suck? I mean, it's only the beginning of the semester and we're already working our butts off.

CAL

(Apathetically. He does not look up.)
Yeah, it's pretty terrible.
(Looking up, he notices how attractive she is. He smiles, then grows friendlier.)
Well, it is good to stay on top of things, now isn't it?

KELLY

(Over anxious.)
I'm Kelly.
(Holding out her hand to be shaken.)

CAL

Hi, Kelly. It's nice to meet you.
   (Shaking her hand.)
I'm Cal.
   (Kelly giggles.)
Did I miss something?

KELLY

   (Giggling.)
Just… Kelly; Cal … Cal; Kelly… Our names just sound a lot alike.

CAL

   (Sarcastically.)
Okay.

KELLY

Mind if I join you?

CAL

   (Anxiously.)
Huh-uh!
   (Then remembering his manners.)
I mean… no, not at all… be my guest.

KELLY

   (Sits down at table.)
Thanks.
   (They study a moment in silence.)
So, Cal, what are you studying?

CAL

Anatomy…

KELLY

Ew, sounds boring.

CAL

...of the female body.
(He smiles.)

KELLY

(Quickly.)
Oh.
(Then getting it.)
Oh!! I see! I was wondering why you seemed so anxious to study.

CAL

Yes, well, the female body is a beautiful thing. It's the one topic I never tire of studying.

KELLY

I'm sure.
(Awkward silence. They study for a few moments. Cal begins glancing at Kelly. She ignores him at first, then begins to quickly glance back at him. Cal's glances turn into stares. Kelly grows increasingly uncomfortable. She scratches her neck. She re-crosses her legs. She crosses her arms; she re-crosses them attempting to cover her chest. She sits awkwardly.)
Hey, buddy, do you mind? You're really starting to creep me out here. How about you keep your eyes on your book?

CAL

Oh, I'm sorry. I just couldn't help noticing how similar you look to the female models in the textbook.
(Turns book as if looking at a centerfold.)

KELLY

Excuse me?!

CAL

The similarity is striking. Care to see for yourself?

KELLY

How dare you!

CAL

What?

KELLY

You little pervert, sitting there undressing me with your eyes.

CAL

Oh, no, no, no!

KELLY

Yeah, whatever. I don't care. Just get back to studying your book instead of studying me, okay?

CAL

(To calm her down.)
Gosh, I'm sorry... I... I didn't mean to offend you. I meant it as a compliment, honest. I would never undress you without your permission.
(She starts to object.)
Wait! Um, I mean, I wouldn't undress you with my eyes.
(Smiles innocently.)
I have nothing but the utmost respect for the female body. I hope you don't think I'm a perv.

KELLY

You know what, dude, I don't care what gets you off. Just mind your own business and let me get back to mine.

CAL

Alright, but I really *did* mean it as a compliment.
(They sit in awkward silence once again. Both go back to their reading. They cast quick glances at one another. Cal flips the pages of his book and somberly turns his attention back to his reading. Kelly begins to feel bad for being so hard on him.)

KELLY

(Apologetically.)
Look, Cal, don't take what I said too personally. Sorry, if I was mean—

CAL

You weren't mean.

KELLY

I really don't think that you're a sex-crazed, testosterone-driven, shallow pig or anything like that.
(Beat.)
Are you?

CAL

No!

KELLY

Of course you aren't! See? I told you so.
(Beat.)
I appreciate your "offensive" compliment.

CAL

Um, well, you're welcome… I guess. You must have shallow, dorky guys like me tell you how pretty you are all the time, right? I bet you get tired of it.

KELLY

You think I'm pretty?

CAL

Of course! And you think I'm shallow and dorky.

KELLY

Of course I don't!

CAL

Well, I just said I was! You were supposed to disagree with me.

KELLY

I'm sorry… I don't think you are any of those things.
 (Their eyes meet and they smile.)

CAL

 (Looks down at book and makes a face.)
Ugh. I have to study the anatomy of the male body now.

KELLY

 (Interested.)
Oh reeeeeeally?

CAL

Not quite as interesting for me.

KELLY

I understand.

CAL

Yep, ain't nothing these models got that I don't have plenty of myself.

KELLY

 (Smirks.)
Right.
 (Kelly looks down at her work and then at Cal. He continues to study with a bored look on his face. Kelly makes frequent glances toward Cal. She strains her neck trying to look over at his book. She scoots her bum on the chair to see better. She drops her pencil; Cal looks up.)
Oh, clumsy me.
 (Cal goes back to his book. Kelly reaches to pick up her pencil; while straining to look over his shoulder, she loses her balance and falls to the floor. Cal jumps up. Kelly stands quickly to compose herself.)

CAL

Are you okay?

KELLY

Yes, yes, I'm fine.
    (Clears throat and smiles.)

CAL

Okay.
    (Kelly sits back down. They begin to study again in silence.)

KELLY

Do you need any help with that? I mean... I, um... had that class last semester and I could help you study if you like?

CAL

No, that's okay. I don't want to offend you again. We should probably stick to our own work.

KELLY

    (Innocently.)
Well, just offering.
    (They study in silence again... thinking.)
Hey, did you hear that?

CAL

What is it?

KELLY

I think I heard someone knocking on the back door of the lobby.

CAL

Oh... I didn't hear anything.
    (Looks down to continue reading.)

KELLY

Sure you did. Someone should go check.
(Cal studies.)
I said, someone should go check!
(She smiles sweetly.)

CAL

(Sarcastically.)
And I guess that someone should be me, huh?

KELLY

Well, if it's not too much trouble…
(She smiles innocently. Cal eyes her suspiciously and sets the book down, pages open, as if setting a trap, then walks offstage. Kelly makes a mad dash for the anatomy book. She sits in Cal's seat, and quickly flips through the pages. She turns the book lengthwise with wide eyes. Cal tiptoes back on stage, and leans over her shoulder.)

CAL

Looking for something…?
(Kelly jumps in her seat and frantically tries to close the book and look as innocent as possible. She smiles.)

KELLY

(Innocently.)
What?

CAL

(Untrustingly.)
Thought you heard knocking on the door, huh?

KELLY

(Guiltily.)
Ummmmm…

CAL

(Taking book from her.)

And you called me a pervert for enjoying my studies?

KELLY

I was just… looking for spare change in the cushions…
  (Standing.)
…no luck here.

CAL

Sure you were…

KELLY

Well, I better get back to my reading. We both know how exciting American politics are.

CAL

  (Sarcastically.)
I don't know. Maybe as fun as looking at nudie pictures in an anatomy book for "educational purposes."
  (He laughs. She gives him a sharp look as they both sit back down. They mind their own business for a few moments. Cal begins to giggle. Kelly gives him a sharp look; eyes meet, and he stops. He does this three times. Kelly grows more playfully "agitated.")

KELLY

Will you please stop that!

CAL

Yeah, sorry.
  (Cal giggles again.)

KELLY

  (Flirtatiously.)
Man, the maturity of some people.

CAL

You know, you're just as bad as I am.

KELLY

Not *as* bad.
(*Their eyes meet and they smile.*)

CAL

You know what? I'm tired of reading. Say… would you like to go back to my place and…

KELLY

Yeah, and…

CAL

…and watch the Discovery Channel with me?

KELLY

The Discovery Channel?

CAL

You see; I heard they were running a special Human Anatomy series tonight.

KELLY

(*Quickly.*)
Part three of a week-long series.

CAL

You're a watcher?
(*She nods.*)
I do believe that it's important for us to have an educated *grasp* on the human anatomy… I could really use the assistance of someone who has had the class before.
(*He stands and moves in closer to her.*)

KELLY

(*Standing.*)
Well, I would do anything to assist a fellow student in need of quality study time.

CAL

(Voice cracking.)
Anything?
(Kelly smiles. They begin to gather their things as they stare seductively at each other. They begin to exit, walking normal pace at first, then quickening to a near run by the time they reach offstage. The Blood Hound Gang song starts to play "You and me baby ain't nothin' but mammals…" as lights begin to fade.)

BLACKOUT

Commander Danny

by Jeremy Kerr
with Aissa Williams

Commander Danny

by Jeremy Kerr with Aissa Williams

THE CHARACTERS

Danny—A young man in his early twenties. He appears to be a nut case.
Merritt—A woman in her late twenties.

THE SCENE

The Setting: The action of the play takes place on a bench in a public park.
The time: The present.

(The stage is dark; we hear music. Something like David Bowie's Space Oddity *pleading "ground control to Major Tom." The lights then come up to reveal a park bench center and a large trashcan stage right. MERRITT sits on the bench, reading. She has an oversized shoulder bag with her containing her lunch. The music fades out when we hear COMMANDER DANNY give out a loud "Weeeee" type yell as he runs on from stage right.)*

DANNY

Weeeee!!
    (He wears work coveralls and a book bag. His shirt is a shiny material that looks like a piece of fabric folded in half with a hole cut for his head, which it is. He is also wearing a belt around the "shirt" with a toy ray-gun tucked into it. On his head he wears a mop bucket as a helmet. He runs to stage left and stops. He places his fingers to his ear to talk into a "cuff microphone" in a very FBI sort of way.)
Gold Leader, this is Red Five: Commander Danny. I've landed safely on Earth and my presence has gone unnoticed.
    (He turns and sees the woman looking at him.)
Gold Leader, strike that last comment from the records.
    (He takes his hand down and gives the woman a fist-to-chest, then fist-in-the-air salute.)
Greetings!

MERRITT

Um… Hi.

DANNY

I am Commander Danny… from the planet Nebali.

MERRITT

Good for you.
    (She goes back to reading her book. He stands watching her until she finally looks up.)
I suppose you want me to take you to my leader now, don't you?

DANNY

    (With excitement.)
Could you?

MERRITT

No.
    (She goes back to reading, which she does frequently when trying to ignore Danny.)

DANNY

Oh. Well. That was a very unkind offer then, wasn't it, Earth Female?

MERRITT

    (Not really caring.)
Yeah. Sorry.
    (He goes back to watching her and again she notices.)
You know, I just wanted a quiet, peaceful day in the park. I really don't have time for this.

DANNY

I am an emissary from another planet! How can you not have time for this?

MERRITT

No, you are a guy with a bucket on his head and a toy gun.

DANNY

What?

(Removes gun from belt.)
This? This is a Class Four Mol-Rec.

MERRITT

A Mol-What?

DANNY

Mol-Rec. Molecular Reconfigure... er.

MERRITT

Ah.

DANNY

It can reconfigure your molecules, turning you into ashes.
(Puts gun back in belt.)

MERRITT

Right.

DANNY

And this?
(Taps helmet.)
This is a helmet. It protects me on space travels... and when I'm on other planets, such as Earth, it translates your language into mine so I can understand you.

MERRITT

Then why can *I* understand *you*?
(He has no answer.)
Yeah, it's a bucket. May I go back to reading my book?

DANNY

Yes.
(She does. He takes off his book bag and opens it. He takes a TV remote control out of it and speaks, rather loudly, into it as a recording device.)
Log One: Earth. Inhabitants: trusting... yet untrusting. Will offer communication, yet will not believe facts. Plant life: green. And brown. With yellows and

oranges and—well, lots of colors. Sky: white. With large areas of blue. Animal life: this could take a while: slugs, birds—

MERRITT

Excuse me, Captain Kirk—

DANNY

Commander Danny.

MERRITT

Riiiight… Anyway, Spock, I really can't concentrate with you being so loud. If you have to talk, could you at least whisper maybe?

DANNY

My deepest apologies.
  (In a very loud whisper.)
Ant-eaters, orangutans, water fowl… which may count as birds… fish—

MERRITT

Okay, you know what? That's still way too loud.

DANNY

I have a Visual Recorder! Should I use that to collect information instead?

MERRITT

Yes. Fine.
  (Danny puts the remote into his pocket and goes back to his book bag and pulls out the handset to a rotary phone. He then begins to walk around pointing it at things as if filming them. At points, he is crawling around on his hands and knees to record things. Finally, he aims it at her and slowly leans in pointing it at her head. She tries to ignore him for a while, then speaks.)
This isn't working, either!

DANNY

I'm sorry. How would the Earth Female propose I gather information?

MERRITT

(Getting up.)
I would propose you gather it someplace else. Like home. Maybe you should go home?
(Danny laughs heartily.)
What? What's so funny?

DANNY

I can't gather information about Earth if I go home to Nebali.
(Still laughing, he goes back to filming things.)

MERRITT

I didn't say anything about Nebali, you freak. I was just saying maybe you should go back to your *house*. Just please quit bothering me. I was here first. I come here every Sunday afternoon to read and I've come to think of this as "my bench." Alright?

DANNY

Even in bad weather?

MERRITT

What?

DANNY

Well, you said you come here *every* Sunday. Does that mean you come here to partake of your books when it is raining?

MERRITT

(Pause.)
Go. Away.
(She sits back down, reading, and he returns his "visual recorder" to the book bag.)

DANNY

Yes.
(He takes a large step away from the bench and stands staring at the woman.)

MERRITT

What are you doing?

DANNY

Observing!

MERRITT

Well, stop it. I'm getting tired of this. Either you leave or I'm going to call the police.

DANNY

(With excitement.)
Ah! The planetary law enforcement!

MERRITT

(Going through her bag.)
I have pepper spray.

DANNY

Ooooo… indigenous spices used as a deterrent! Lovely!

MERRITT

(Unable to find pepper spray.)
Listen, Captain D's, at least stop staring at me, okay?

DANNY

Yes.
(He spins on his heels to face away from her. He notices the trashcan and then crosses to it. He clears his throat to get her attention and she looks.)
Well… I'm leaving!
(He waves goodbye to her; she waves back sarcastically.)
What's that?!
(He points past her and she looks. He ducks down behind the trashcan. When she looks back, she doesn't see him. She gives a relieved sigh then begins going through her bag again, taking out a sandwich and drink. He peers over the top of the trashcan and when she isn't looking his way, he picks it up in front of him, hiding himself in a very

cartoon-like way with his legs visible. As she begins to eat, he crosses with the can behind her and sets it down to her left, still crouching behind it. He waits a moment, then picks it up again, coming closer to her. He sets it down, crouching, and takes the TV remote/voice recorder out of his pocket.)
The Earth female, Subject Zero-Zero-One, is now engaged in introducing fuels into the body. She has a sandwich, a bottle—

MERRITT

Danny!
(They both stand.)

DANNY

Yes?

MERRITT

Go away!

DANNY

Why?

MERRITT

Because this isn't normal social behavior. I'm a normal girl trying to read, and you're some loony off his medication who's bothering the hell out of me! Now, this is my bench. This is *my* Sunday bench. This is *my* book that I 'm reading on *my* Sunday bench in *my* section of the park! Now leave me alone. Go home to *your* padded walls… to *your* straight jacket… and stop bothering me!!

DANNY

(Speaking into recorder.)
Subject Zero-Zero-One shows signs of agitation.

MERRITT

"Signs of agitation"? I'm pissed off! Now go!

DANNY

(Beat.)

Do you know the difference between the Class Three Mol-Rec and the Class Four, which I have?

(Takes gun from belt and looks at it.)

MERRITT

No. And you know what? I don't care!

DANNY

The Class Three doesn't have a stun setting.

MERRITT

Aww… how terrible. Now leave me alone!

DANNY

The Class Four does.

MERRITT

That's wonderful. Why don't you take your Class Four and—

(Danny points the gun at her and pulls the trigger. We hear the sound of a laser gun firing. The woman freezes in her tracks, perfectly still. Danny returns the gun to his belt and speaks with his fingers to his ear again.)

DANNY

Red Four, this is Red Five. Requesting assistance for subject relocation.

(Another man enters from right, dressed identical to Danny. They salute and Danny points to the woman. They tilt her over and pick her up like a statue and exit left with her.)

BLACKOUT

The Playwrights

Rachel Jones currently teaches English at an elementary school in Suwon, South Korea. She graduated from GWU in 2004 with a major in English. She has written various pieces for 24 HOURS. She considers herself to be, in many cases, "as unique as the characters she creates." Her unusual way of seeing the world lends great power to her writing, which includes other forms besides writing for the theater.

Carrie Cranford is a theater alum of GWU. A current resident of Charlotte, North Carolina, she returns regularly to participate in our 24 HOURS event. An accomplished actress, Carrie has been seen most recently in an evening of one-acts in a Charlotte-area theater.

Jeremy Kerr is currently Guest Artist for the GWU Theater. He has been acting professionally for more than five years, touring in nearly thirty states with various theater companies. When not on the road, he lives in Shelby, North Carolina, lending his talents and skills to GWU Theater through his acting and writing. He feels that writing for 24 HOURS has really helped hone his abilities; at his age, he wants to "get it done in as few drafts as possible so he can get home and get to bed."

Amanda Miller is a University Fellow at GWU, where her academic pursuits have provided her a reputation for high achievement. Her participation in 24 HOURS was part of a long-term commitment to experiencing new things. We are honored to have had Amanda as part of the team.

Meg Elliot is an English major at GWU in her senior year. She is a lovely red-haired girl who is capable of stealing your heart away, if you do not guard against it, as she has done to so many young men here at GWU. We all expect Meg to do great things as she continues to explore her writing talents.

Tiffany Stephens is currently a senior at GWU. She is from Wilmington, North Carolina and will graduate with a double major in Theater Arts and Spanish. She plans to pursue an MFA in Stage Directing with hopes of directing professionally. She has directed several one-act plays and acted in many plays, to include the title role in *The House of Bernarda Alba.*

George Harrison Hendricks IV is a writer/actor who currently lives in Atlanta, Georgia. He performed onstage regularly until recently. After discovering his gift for writing, he realized that he prefers making up the words more than memorizing them. He's currently unemployed and more than a little curious as to where his next paycheck is coming from. He looks forward to more opportunities to collaborate with theater folk and hopes to see his work performed as much as possible.

Brad Archer is a double major in Theater Arts and Spanish at GWU in his sophomore year. His production credits include work as an actor, director, and writer. His first appearance on the college stage was as Tarleton in G.B. Shaw's *Misalliance.* He dreams of one day opening his own theater. In his free time, he enjoys smoking his pipe, listening to sad music, and writing in his journal like an adolescent girl.

Donovan Craft graduated from GWU in 2003 with a BA in Theater Arts. He returned recently to GWU to study theology in the Christopher M. White School of Divinity. His play *True Love* was presented in the very first 24 HOURS held at GWU; it is also the only script taken from that first event.

Wendy Shockley graduated from Gardner-Webb University in 2003 with a major in Communication Studies. She presently works with the FOX Network in Charlotte, North Carolina and WCCB News. She also keeps busy as a wedding photographer and videographer. Her stage appearances at GWU include Catesby in *Richard III*, the mute in *The Fantasticks,* and Tina in *The Search For Signs of Intelligent Life in the Universe.*

Pamela Darnell is a senior at GWU finishing her degree in Public Relations with minors in Spanish and Psychology. If her aspirations to become a Publicly Relating Spanish Psychologist do not work out, she hopes to go into PR for a nonprofit organization. Pamela stumbled into theater on an "I'll try out if you try out" bet with a friend. When she's not busy trying to change the world, she enjoys good conversations, old jazz music, Gerbera daisies, dangly earrings, and putting prepositions at the end of sentences.

Noelle DeLozier is a sophomore Theater Arts major at Gardner-Webb University with a minor in Religious Studies. Her first appearance on the college stage was as Hypatia in G.B. Shaw's *Misalliance*. When not at college, she lives in Maryland with her family and enjoys being a camp counselor in the summers.

Micheal S. Pardue is a Theater Arts major at Gardner-Webb University. He has directed in each of our 24 HOURS events and written for all but one. He has written a number of other plays including *She's Not the First, Fire Prevention*, and *Curiosity Kills*. He is happily married and is excited by the success his writing is bringing him.

Stephanie Faile is a freshman journalism major at GWU with a great love for the arts. She's spent seven wonderful years working in theater prior to her experience at Gardner-Webb—two years as an actor in the Lancaster Community Playhouse and five years as an actor/dancer/technician at Narroway Productions in Fort Mill, South Carolina. Her hobbies are writing, reading, and spending time with friends.

Amber McGinnis Jackson graduated from GWU with a double major in Theater Arts and Religious Education. She presently lives in Boiling Springs, North Carolina with her husband. Amber is currently preparing for graduate studies towards an MFA in directing. She wishes to thank her husband for appreciating her quirky sense of humor, her friends for Saturday nights at Denny's, and her parents for not minding that their daughter's play was the "naughtiest" in the 24 HOURS production.

Michael Mitteer is a junior at GWU with a double major in Business and the Theater Arts. He has written several lengthy dramatic works and hopes to see his longer work on the stage in years to come. He admires the writings of Bertolt Brecht, traces of which shows up in Mike's own writing. When asked about his "slightly twisted sense of humor," Mike responds that it's "just a rumor."

Aissa Williams currently lives in Orlando, Florida. She recently moved from South Carolina where she was an assistant teacher at a Montessori school. She will soon be transferring her academic credits to the University of Central Florida, where she will be pursuing a degree in Communication Studies.

The Cast and Production Teams

EQUAL OPPORTUNITY EMPLOYER was directed by Amber Jackson, and starred Matt Winning, Carrie Cranford, and Elaine Bell.

EXHIBIT 4 was directed by Alison Rinehardt, and starred Pamela Darnell, Matthew Fraiser, Hannah O' Daniel, and Jeff Houser.

THE DOCTOR IS OUT was directed by Amanda Murphy, and starred Brian Lewis and Alison Blackwell.

GOOD HELP was written for 24 HOURS, but was deemed too complicated to produce technically within the time restraints of this performance event. It was subsequently produced in Gardner-Webb University's New Plays Festival 2004. That production was directed by Amanda Murphy, and starred Dave Hawes as the Doctor and Danny Guynn as the hunchback.

PAPER FOOTBALL was directed by Micheal S. Pardue, and starred Dustin McMillan, Sky DeBoever, and Kate McNerney.

TRUE LOVE was directed by Micheal S. Pardue, and starred Wendy Shockley and Ryan Stamey.

MISS TRANQUILITY was directed by Amber Jackson, starred Pamela Darnell and Brandon Juhaish, and featured Liz Nichols and Kelly Navey.

IN THE BEGINNING was written and directed by George Harrison Hendricks IV. Mr. Hendricks also played the leading role of this mostly one-man show. It featured Nathan Klein and Constance Anhalt in the auxiliary roles.

FORTRESS OF SOLITUDE was directed by Tiffany Stephens, and starred Matt Winning and Pam Darnell.

SOCIAL DISTORTION was directed by Brad Archer, and starred Alesia Hinson and Caleb Moore.

STUDY TIME was directed by Micheal S. Pardue, and starred Rachel Jones and Matt Marlowe.

IT'S THE THOUGHT THAT COUNTS was directed by Brad Archer, and starred Dustin McMillan and Heather Bartlett.

COMMANDER DANNY was directed by Amanda Murphy, and starred Jeremy Kerr and Rachel Jones.

978-0-595-35066-7
0-595-35066-6